Pilgrims

with Credit Cards

Asifa Kanji

D. Drury & Sons, Publishers

London ✦ Berkeley ✦ Hilo ✦ Ashland

This is my personal story. The views expressed in
this book are the authors' alone.

Inquiries and comments may be sent to:
ddruryandsonspub@gmail.com

ISBN-13: 978-1-7350623-0-3

To my mum, with love and gratitude.
Your spirit continues to hug me.

A pilgrimage is a journey of the heart.

-Peter Matthiessen

Contents

The Camino del Norte

El Camino de Santiago
del Norte y Primitivo

— 0 Camiño do Norte / El Camino del Norte / The Northern Way
Le Chemin du Nord / Nördlicher Pilgerweg / O Caminho do Norte / Il Camino del Nord
— 0 Camiño Primitivo / El Camino Primitivo / The Primitive Way
Le Chemin Primitif / Der Ursprüngliche Pilgerweg / O Camiño Primitivo / Il Camino Primitivo

Camino maps courtesy Ideas Peregrinas www.ideasperegrinas.es

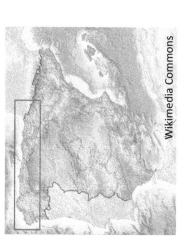

Wikimedia Commons

In the Beginning

"I want to do something holy, in a secular kind of way," David says, "And be among pilgrims."

"Come again?"

"One of my dreams is to walk the Camino," he tells me over a glass of wine.

"The whaaaat?"

"The Camino de Santiago, in Spain -- you know, the walk to the tomb of St. James."

Images of crowded trails and smelly hostels run through my head. "Why?" I ask.

He can't really articulate this draw from deep within. Maybe it has to do with being a fallen away Catholic -- kind of like, "I'm sorry Catholic God, but with Science on my side, I stopped believing in you as a smart-ass kid of 14 . . . but I'm still drawn to what is sacred."

Now he is a smart-ass kid of 67 with even more knowledge crammed into his cerebral cortex. He is reading every tome, encyclopedia and manuscript he can lay his hands on, just inhaling the myths, legends and histories about this ancient walk.

"Did you know . . . ?" his favorite opening line, is already popping up in our dinner-time conversations. He then regales me with the latest. Being erudite is what he does best. Fortunately or not, my brain is a colander, eager to receive learnings which then easily drain away. This makes us the perfect couple, since he can regale me with historical stories over and over, as he is wont to do, and I am always just as entertained as I was the first time.

It is one thing learning about the history of the Camino over dinner conversations, but the very idea of walking hundreds of miles, carrying a backpack, sleeping in hostels, just to visit the tomb of some Catholic saint, does not make me want to rush and pack my bags. I'd done enough sleeping in hostels in our recent Peace Corps service. My preferred spiritual journey would be to climb a mountain and sleep under the Milky Way.

"So were you thinking of doing this on your own?" I ask.

"Not at all. I want you to come with me. We have always done big things together, and this would be a meaningful experience for both of us."

Wow! He really wants me to share this journey with him. The thought tugs at my heart. Maybe it would be a good thing for us to do. We have taken other walking holidays and have loved them. But on most of those, someone else schlepped our luggage or we stayed in cozy bed and breakfasts.

It will be a different kind of adventure. Come on, just go Asifa, my instinct prompts. *Don't be ridiculous, do you really want to walk fifteen miles a day, every day?* says the other voice in my head. *What a beautiful invitation from your husband,* my heart murmurs. *He really wants you to go with him. Besides, you can do it at a more leisurely pace.*

"Okay, I'll come," I announce in my princess voice. "But no dorms. I will only sleep in a private room with an en-suite bathroom." He agrees.

We also agree that if the going gets tough, I will head for the beach, get massages, listen to the ocean, eat garlic langoustines, sip wine, and wait there for him. Okay, so we don't discuss what I will do while at the beach. But I don't see any problem with using my credit card, or taking time to listen to the waves and sip colorful drinks with paper umbrellas floating in them. While I have never been tempted to take vows of poverty, chastity or obedience, I do love a good adventure.

That's it. The decision is made. We are going and I'm on board. Off with the tiara and on with the hiking boots.

The anticipation of the pilgrimage takes me on a fantasy trip. Maybe I'll come back a wise old crone who will not be afraid to dance barefoot under the light of the moon with a crown of wild flowers in my hair. I will sip dew drops, for wise old crones do that, don't they?

Sipping dew drops? Dancing barefoot? Really? my brain pipes up. *With your creaky old bones?*

Yeah, but surely walking a hundred and thirty miles on the pilgrimage trail will transform me.

We'll see!

3

I am browsing online for my Camino wardrobe when David gives me that professorial look.

"Did you know that centuries before St. James and Jesus were even born, Spain was crisscrossed with pilgrim paths?"

"Mmm, that's interesting," I say. "But just look at these weigh-nothing, breathable, SPF50, quick dry shirts." I try to show him the ads on my phone. He barely looks up.

"Parts of the Camino del Norte, the route we are taking, follow the Roman roads which were used to conquer the north of Spain in the time of Caesar Augustus. Even earlier, pagan pilgrims followed the path of the Milky Way, going west to the Altar of the Sun at Finisterre, the end of the earth."

Quite automatically, "Oh really," spills out of my mouth. "Do you think we should buy new boots? We should do it now, just so we can break them in, don't you think?" I continue my part of the conversation, which is much more important than derelict Roman roads.

And thus, each of us prepares for our long walk on one of the less traveled Caminos, the del Norte. It starts in Irun in France, but we'll be picking it up in Ribadeo, where the Norte enters the province of Galicia. This first time around, we are going to test our stamina on the 130 mile walk to Santiago de Compostela.

What to bring? How many pairs of shoes and which ones is my biggest quandary. I need something I can walk around in, something that will look sassy, but also something that will take up as little space as possible. What clothes? My crinkly pretty top is winking at me. "Go on take me. You won't regret it." I pack, unpack, and test the rucksack on my back. Out with the bathing suit and fancy shoes. Out with the crinkly top. I'm trying to keep the whole thing down to 12 pounds. In the end, it dawns on me, I can take just one change of clothes.

We go out on our first practice walk in the hills behind our home with full packs on our backs. Within an hour, I feel the arch drop in my right foot. I must have injured the fascia.

Ouch!

Here we are about to embark on a 130 mile trek, and we are due to leave in just a few days. Our tickets are non-refundable.

Let the adventure begin!

Day 1: Ribadeo to Villa Martín Grande

As we approach Ribadeo on the bus, my heart starts banging against my rib cage with such fury that I'm afraid it will burst out. My brain drags me into a murky quagmire of *I am going to die*, or worse still, *I will have to have my foot amputated by a farmer, with an axe and no anesthetic, in the middle of a cow pasture.* I am drowning in guilt for ruining my husband's dream. I clutch my water bottle like a child hugging her tatty old teddy, for comfort. *I will be OK. I will be OK.* I repeat. *David cares for me and together we'll do what's best.* Still fear reigns. I can barely breathe. We get off the bus to look for our room. I am a walking ghost, going through the motions, trying to just breathe and hide my anxiety. The reality of my planters fasciitis and the 130 mile walk ahead is beginning to sink in.

David is skipping around, almost dancing for joy, poking me, trying to get me to play. "Cheer up, we are here!" He is bursting with excitement like a child who has been good all year, and now finally it is Christmas day. He indeed has been good, looking up the exact route, scrutinizing the elevations, the terrain, the availability of drinking water and cafes. He has booked places to sleep and mapped out how far we would walk each day. And now here we are, Camino virgins.

"Before we take on the 12 miles tomorrow, let's fuel-up with a big breakfast," he says, drooling at the *perigrino* -- pilgrim -- menu of ham, eggs, bread and coffee, outside many a café that we pass.

I smile, but the voices in my head are getting louder. *There's no way you can eat early in the morning, let alone walk right after. Maybe you shouldn't go. You'll ruin his trip. Quit now and go to the beach.*

I keep walking, as though the walking will pound the fear out of me. The surrounding buildings look as tired and worn-down as I feel. There's hardly anybody around, save a barista or two looking bored behind their counters.

Finally, I find my voice. "I have absolutely no faith that my body will come through for me," I say, tears rolling down my cheeks. David puts his arms around me and hugs me closely.

Buck up Asifa, it's not just about you. The voice in my head changes its tune.

"If we skip breakfast and start really early, it would buy me extra time, in case my feet need it. I would rather have just a power bar to go for breakfast," I tell David. By now, he is doing all he can to appease me.

I pop two sleeping pills to knock myself out. At 6 am, our alarms shake us awake. Surprise! It is still the middle of the night outside. This is the third week of August, but the dawn does not dawn until 7:08 and the sun will rise at 7:38 am. At least that's what my smarter-than-me phone says. Who knew that Galicia was on the very edge of Spain's time zone, and thus the late sunrise? We drift back to sleep until the sun smacks us in the face. I give my bad foot the royal treatment -- a massage with loads of ibuprofen gel -- and bind both feet in special tape. We repack our packs so that they are perfectly balanced. After taking two pills, I slip a film canister full of anti-inflammatories into my pocket.

David sacrifices his bacon and eggs breakfast for instant oatmeal made with hot tap water, forsaking the icing-filled, sticky buns our hostess has left in the common room. *Sticky Willies*, that's what I called these things when I was in English boarding school. I have to try one for old time's sake. With the first bite, my whole mouth is slimed by the sugary icing. Yuk! Gargle, spit. Gargle, spit. Out the door we go, and into the morning mist we disappear.

We are on our way.

Mountains, villages, cows and trees are soft phantoms with stories waiting to unfold. Blurry cornfields sharpen ever so slowly. I love the untidy clumps of curbside pink and purple wild flowers. Gradually farmers awake, and not long after, the chug-chugging of a tractor here and there rattles the morning. Barnyard smells mix with the heaviness of damp hay. Eucalyptus infuses the air. The sun, a bloated pink ball of cotton candy, warms the mist, lifting it up, up and away. If there are any birds, they are quiet, and the butterflies have yet to wake

8

up. The mellow mood, the freshness of the morning breeze puts a spring into my step. I am witness to the dawning of a new day.

A man with a backpack approaches, just getting into his stride. He smiles as we photograph each other in front of the Camino marker. "This is our first day," I say. He nods but keeps going, leaving in his wake a "*Buen Camino*".

A cluster of five early twenties-ish walkers sails right past us. "*Buen Camino!*" More *Buen Camino* greetings roll past. I am the old lady with the hat, driving way below speed limit with both hands on the steering wheel. Still, I am walking and not in pain. For now, my foot has been whipped into shape and walks like this is completely the most normal thing to do. Here's to just saying Yes to painkillers.

A German teacher catches up with us, and slows his pace to ours. "I have walked this many times and all the other Caminos too," he says. If he had a ribbon pinned to his breast for each time he'd walked a camino, he would resemble a five star general. "A beautiful walk, cheap accommodations, good food and bottomless glasses of wine. What's not to like?" he says about this particular Camino. Like a medieval pilgrim, he had stepped out of his door at home in Bavaria, and started walking. It has taken him several years to get this far, as at the end of each summer he has to return home to teach. Each year he starts walking from where he left off.

Much further along, I'm about to ask David at an unmarked junction, "Should we take the high or the low road?" A voice from behind startles me. "When in doubt, always go uphill."

The voice belongs to a mean, lean walking machine from Cleveland Ohio, who had started in Irun, France, a few weeks ago. He and his wife have already walked more than 300 miles, averaging 15 to 20 miles per day. This last hundred miles is their home stretch. "The first week was hard," she says, "but now these legs are totally in tune." Their Coppertone legs are moving at four miles an hour with such ease, like gazelles cantering. I wonder if I will ever reach that level of grace and beauty. Still, I am walking and not in pain.

Villamartin Grande, Albergue Tentempe

"I did it. I did it!" I dance a very short jig for finishing the first eleven miles on my own two feet, powered by Ibuprofen. The last big hill to our albergue, our lodging at Villamartin Grande almost did me in, but it doesn't matter, because I made it. David and I clink our beer glasses like they're celebratory glasses of Don Perignon. We have the whole afternoon and evening in this hamlet where the café of our albergue is the only attraction.

Hiking poles and a motley collection of backpacks lean up against a corner, most with scallop shells dangling from their frames. The pilgrim's calling card. My brand new pack sparkles like a new button among them. All those people who passed us up are sitting out on the terrace, sipping coffee, licking ice cream cones or enjoying a beer with their *boccadillo,* a ham and cheese sandwich of sorts. For them this is just a watering hole. They have five more miles to go to reach Lourenzá, where cheap pilgrim *albergues* -- hostels -- with communal kitchens, showers and dorms abound. I am thrilled that we do not have to walk further.

Carmen, our hostess, brings us a plate of home baked cakes and me a Ziplock bag full of ice to chill my feet. "What time would you like dinner?" she asks. "My mama is cooking a delicious meal for you." Mama does not speak English, but her nods and laughter speak loads. The only other person staying over is a Czech guy, whom I had seen on the trail with just a tiny day pack.

"Do you not even carry a change of clothes?" I ask Mr Czechia. He laughs as he points to a large metal suitcase, its handle choked with labels. "Correos delivered my bag. It's very cheap. You should czech it out."

"How much?" I ask

"30 Euros, for delivery to all stops to Santiago."

"Correos, the Spanish Postal Service? They pick up and deliver backpacks?" It takes me all of two minutes to write down the details. For the first time, I know I will complete this walk.

As we pilgrim watch, an American from South Carolina joins us. "What I would give for a bowl of noodles," he says, trying to inhale the essence of Ramen noodles that a couple is cooking on their private camping stove nearby.

"Instant Ramen noodles. Really?" I ask. "That would be better than ham and cheese sandwiches?" To me Ramen noodles have the nutritional value of wet cardboard, with a lot of salt sprinkled on it.

"South Korea has been my home for many years. I miss eating noodles." He teaches English literature. Walking the Camino was his fiftieth birthday present to himself. A cheap Spanish vacation, he thought. From the guidebooks that lured him, he believed he would be spending €5 a day in albergues with the promise of delicious, wholesome, cheap meals. The reality has been just a little different.

"The race for beds was the last thing I expected," the American says. Evidently the first-come first-served albergues fill up within minutes of their doors opening. Some walkers leave at 4 am, virtually jog the 15 to 20 kilometers to be at the hostel by 9 am. Any dawdler would have to walk to the next town, possibly another 10 or 15 kilometers away, in search of a bed.

"So what are the albergues like?" I ask.

"I don't mind the snoring, but these dorms are like tombs. The window, if there is one, is invariably too tiny to make any difference. Every molecule of air has been breathed thrice over, has been farted, coughed and sneezed into. I'm done with dark and dank dorms," Mr. South Carolina tells us.

That is it. If I had any delusions left about being a part of the Camino family that sleeps, bathes, and eats communally, they evaporate in less than a nanosecond. Yes, I might miss out on a surprise experience or a deeper friendship, but for right now, I'll settle for unmemorable comfort.

The noodle kids are slurping their lunch. The American can't stand it any longer, abandons his *bocadillo* and leaves to continue walking. Ramen noodles don't speak to me in the same way. I want a big plate of fresh broccoli or an artichoke, some steamed baby kale sprinkled with feta and balsamic vinegar, or string beans with almonds and garlic. Hell, I'll even be happy with plain old boiled veggies. We go to the counter and buy the only choice we have, a ham and cheese sandwich.

Day 2: Villa Martín Grande to Lourenzá

Diaphanous fog, lifting and falling.

Forest trails, climbing and descending.

The air is crisp, cool and Eucalyptus scented.

I dance to the dawn of the new day.

I hear footfalls right beside me.

I turn my head, but nobody is there.

Who dances with me?

Is it Saint James?

Nah, not likely.

But the footfalls, they persist, but no footprints do I see.

Footprints! That's the title of the poem printed on fake stained-glass that hung in my mother's flat. It is something about the Lord walking with you, leaving no footprints. I read it once and dismissed it as my mum's penchant for collecting signs of Godly presence. She truly believed that God walked with her, holding her, keeping her safe. If she fell, which she frequently did, it was her own carelessness. The fact that she had broken no bones was God's grace. The poem reflected her faith.

The image of God having feet, and noisy ones at that, conjures up Humpty Dumpty, with his rather bulbous belly balanced on short spindly legs. God as Humpty Dumpty? With thoughts like that, no way was God going to hang out with me.

"Shame on you," my mum pipes up. "You haven't changed one bit, have you? Who do you think is holding you upright and supporting you as you walk? Tell me that." Her voice is as real as if she is walking right next to me.

She would have approved this pilgrim's journey. If she could have, she would have walked it. I can see her dressed in a white robe with a hood covering her silver hair, silently praising the Lord while, with every step, her forefinger and thumb gently pull on the prayer beads of her *tasbi*. *Allahu Akbar*. *Allahu Akbar*. *Allahu Akbar*. God is Great. God is great.

Arthritis and bunions had twisted and deformed her feet. Her toes, instead of lying flat, were piled on top of each other, making walking a major challenge, but it never stopped her. She looked on life as a crucible, in which pain and suffering were the fires that purified her of sins. That, in turn, bought her a seat at God's feet for all eternity, her life's goal. To that end, she took on the problems of the sick, the aged and the poor. She bathed them, she fed them, and she held them close to her heart.

I tell David about the footfalls. "It's my Mum, I just know it. She is walking alongside me as my guardian angel, my companion holding me and keeping me safe."

"Nice image," he says. I catch his smirky smile. I know he's thinking that these sounds have a more logical explanation, like a loose strap banging on my pack or something like that.

I wish I hadn't opened my mouth.

Lourenzá

"No sir, we don't show your reservations," the girl at the desk tells us in the gentlest tone, the lines on her forehead scrunched in puzzlement. She double checks the big book as well as the computer. We fumble with our phones, looking for a confirmation number.

"Oh no, we booked the wrong date," we realize, and today there is no room at the inn. Without any prompts, she starts calling other albergues. David is pulling up one of his many Camino apps to search for options.

"No private rooms anywhere, they are all full," she says. I peek into one of the dorms. Eight bunk beds, stacked two high, crowd the room. It looks clean, and we are here early enough to grab the corner beds, closest to the window. Sort of like getting a corner condo with only one shared wall. I suppose for one night, we could slum it. Better than having to walk to the next town. Just that thought sends a sharp pain up my foot. A rude reminder that it is time to take two more Ibuprofen.

"I have one more place I can try, but it is a little further out of town."

Anxiety, my old foe, pops up to embrace me. Before I fall into its arms, the young lady, holding the mouthpiece to her chest, says, "They have one room for 30 Euros."

We take it.

Pensíon Casa Gloria

I limp to Casa Gloria. Nobody is around. We poke our heads into an open door. It's a bakery, not a pensíon. Are we at the wrong address? My poor feet are so ready to give up, but the smell of cinnamon, vanilla and baking pumps energy into me. An elderly man comes out in his apron.

"Casa Gloria?"

"Si, Si,"

"Tenemos una reservación," we stumble.

He smiles, nods and gives us each an apple turnover, still warm from the oven. "Wait in the garden. Room is not ready." We flop down under an arbor of kiwi fruit begging to be picked, as are the nearby very pregnant pear and apple trees. Plenty of temptation, no serpents, just that little voice that prompts, "Surely they won't miss one. Go on, pluck it."

The pensíon and the bakery are family-owned and run. The daughter stops by to tell us our room is ready. Yes, she will be more than happy to help us make our onward reservations and call Correos to arrange the pickup of my backpack. She personally delivers a baggie full of ice for my feet. The guest wing has a fully equipped kitchen where I ogle a plateful of cakes and pastries. "Help yourself," she says and I do. Never mind walking the Camino, maybe I'll just stay here for the next few weeks and eat home baked cake.

A young woman leans on her mop and in beautiful English chats with us. She is from Venezuela. She speaks French and Portuguese as well and has been to college. "How did you end up here as a cleaning lady?" I ask. After all, this is Noplace, Spain. "I'd expect to find a young, smart, woman like you in Madrid or Barcelona."

"I came to Mondeñedo to buy a mortuary, but the deal did not work out."

"A mortuary?"

"I am a trained embalmer. I studied in Paris under Jean Monceau, the guy who embalmed Lady Di and Jacques Cousteau's body."

My eyes light up, but before I can ask more questions, she asks, "Would you like to come to my house?"

"Yes please." We arrange to meet her at 6 pm.

This is only day two of our walking. I am stoked. Too stoked to nap. Our private bathroom has a skylight and a soaking tub. But before I can allow myself to soak, we must do laundry. With just one change of clothes, washing them by hand is part of the daily routine. Within twenty minutes of checking in, we turn any guest room into a tenement, hanging knickers, socks, shirts and pants to dry, anywhere and everywhere we can. With the washing done, I am too hot to soak. I put my feet on ice, sit back on the bed, and make the first entry into my Camino journal.

"Serendipity took us by the hand and brought us to Casa Gloria."

Rested, revived and renewed, we set out to explore Lourenzá. We let ourselves into a Benedictine monastery that is over a thousand years old, its façade designed by the same architect who built the cathedral in Santiago. Music is wafting out the door. Nobody is there, except for the organ player. I sit and listen, enjoying the coolness these stone walls provide. David plays sleuth, trying to figure out who the saints in each of the naves are. This one has his foot on the dragon and a spear in his hand, therefore he must be . . ..

A bank of electronic vigil candles draws my attention. I slip a coin into the slot. A little red wavy flame lights up and flickers. I put in another coin and a second one lights up. This is holy Bingo. If I get three to light up in a row, will I win a divine jackpot?

I wonder how long they stay lit before they reset themselves. It is not as romantic as lighting a real candle, but then this is probably more ecological and certainly more fun for a heathen such as myself. I lift my gaze to the stone figure carved into the wall, wondering what favors this saint would grant me.

"This is St. Rochus -- the saint against Pestilence," a voice from behind me says. The music director has stopped playing and has come up to join me. Of course, David starts asking all kinds of questions about the saints and, before we know it, we get more art history and who-to-pray-to-for-what than we bargain for. I go along nodding and smiling. Who knew there is a saint in charge of pestilence? I had lit three candles to him -- and wonder if he might be in charge of plantar fasciitis too. Cure me please, dear saint, I beg as earnestly as I can.

The Embalmer

"This is the first place I have been able to call my own," the embalmer says. In the dining room, she throws the enormous wooden windows open with relish and a sense of freedom. Her spirits soar and float in the sky like birds catching a thermal, just enjoying the ride.

She drowns the traffic noise with salsa music. "No boyfriend. No roommates. Just me." It is with a tinge of envy that I follow her around as she shows us the flat she has just moved into. Quilts and cushions splash color on the mattress in one corner of the floor. She speaks of her plans to create a craft room.

I have never had my own flat to do with as I please. David and I got married right out of college. I find myself creating my own fantasy abode in her space, mentally filling it with bookshelves, artwork and oriental rugs. My Moroccan brass table would fit perfectly in front of the sofa. "What a fabulous place this is. You are so lucky," I say as my mind continues to decorate her walls and rooms.

In a kitchen that creaks with age, the old grout peeling away, we slice tomatoes, cheese, and very large garlic-stuffed mushrooms. We slice the baguettes and uncork a bottle of wine. She opens several packages of ham.

"Salud!"

"What drew you to embalming?" I couldn't hold the question in any longer.

"I was always intrigued about death, since childhood. I loved murder mysteries, and I would hang around the mortuary in Venezuela. I can't tell you why. As soon as I could, I moved to

Paris to study under Jean Monceau." She's quiet for a long moment.

"Bodies are often still warm, and the children, they break my heart. It is quite an art to make a person look like they are peacefully asleep, especially if they die in an accident."

"Have you ever thought about writing your own murder mysteries?"

The evening sparkles with conversation and wine. Too soon, we have to take our leave, for we have much to prepare for our dawn departure to Monteñedo. My poor foot aches. I need ice, Ibuprofen and fresh bindings. Starting tomorrow, I will surrender the contents of my pack to Correos to deliver to our next stop.

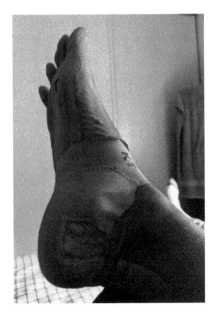

At the pensíon, Papa tells us to beware. "Don't take the new road, the new Camino. Yes, it is shorter. Yes, you'll see spectacular scenery when you get to the top of the mountain. Yes, it's a beautiful walk. BUT it is straight up, and a meteorological disaster."

I have visions of meteors from outer space pummeling us.

"The fog and rain funnel in from the coast," he tells us. Apparently, they drape and drench the mountain, stealing the views from the pilgrims and making the trail very dangerous. "Take the original way, which is now called the Alternativo," he advises.

Day 3: Lourenzá to Mondeñedo

There is something about walking away from a little town while it is still asleep that silences my chatterbox brain. As David and I step deeper into the forest, swaddled in the dawn's mist, I'm imbued with expectations. Maybe I'll discover a secret, or encounter some danger. Something mysterious might cross my path. How will the day unwrap itself?

Today the only thing in my pack is my water bladder. It is so light, I am prancing along. My feet, having rested all night, numbed by painkillers and bound by tape, are feeling normal. We had stuffed all our combined gear into David's pack and left it for Correos to pick-up and deliver. He unfurled his foldable-into-nothing daypack and filled it with the day's essentials.

As we saunter through the forest, I hear the footfalls. I look. There are no footprints.

"Hi Mum," I murmur.

I remember how alienated I felt from her while she was alive. I don't remember her ever hugging me, but in death my love for her abounds. And here she is walking alongside me. *Nobody forgives like a mother*, I think.

"Thank you mum. I miss you so much." My eyes moisten and I swallow to calm that lump in my throat.

"I never listened when you were around, but I am ready now. Will you help me become wise and forgiving and compassionate?"

She remains quiet. It's silly that I should ask her, as I know exactly what she would say. She repeated it all through my life, like a broken record.

"Stop wasting your energy searching for wisdom. Start doing for others, especially the poor and needy, the rejected, the sick and the aged. That is all that really counts."

Indeed, she dedicated her life to doing just that. I had long written off her doing good as purely self serving -- it was her passport to heaven. She kept tally of all the families she helped -- these were her stamps to prove she had done enough good to be allowed through the Pearly Gates.

"I'm sorry mum, I didn't mean to dis you." I fear that she will stop walking with me. Those footfalls would evaporate into the ether.

But then a whisper of a voice comes from inside of me.

Searching for wisdom is like looking for unicorns. It's not to be found. If you are present and awake, the earth will open its soul to you, and like magic, you will feel the presence of grace. Your heart will overflow when the bird says good morning, or when the butterfly stops to kiss a flower, or when the mist rises ever so gently, to welcome you to a new day. Being wise means being aroused, feeling, hearing, smelling and being touched by the present moment.

How true that is. I have been feeling that subliminal connection since we stepped out at dawn. I am awake. I am floating in a heavenly realm, where every wild flower is nodding hello.

I jump when I hear an urgent voice.

"Watch out! Cow poop on the trail." It is David.

That dream evaporates. I pay attention to the muck-filled trail. It is only five miles from Lourenzá to Mondeñedo. Too soon the forest trail spurts us out onto a rural byway, one so narrow that the tips of my fingers can touch the ancient stone walls of the farm dwellings on either side. Ageing *horreos* -- weathered wooden sheds, perched high upon granite pillars -- are just begging to be photographed. Some of them date back to the sixteenth century. It was in these that farmers kept the harvest safe from rot and rodents. Today, most of them stand in the fields as dilapidated monuments to a time gone by.

The village is a ghost town, except for the battalions of strutting roosters behind chain mail fences, clucking at us with curiosity. People must live here, for I see fat electric wires crawling up the stone walls, and television antennas and dishes on roofs. Maybe the locals are catching up on their rest. I can't begin to imagine what the shrill cacophony of this choir of roosters could do to one's sleep, especially at four in the morning.

The solid stone homes speak of family dramas, happy times, desperate times, back-breaking work, and smoky fireplaces. I realize these are modern families, using modern farming techniques who are living here now. But still, I stand quietly, just to absorb the history, and pay my respects to the ancients on whose shoulders today's Galician families stand. How I love traveling through Spain on foot.

As we leave the village, the tiny rural road widens. We hear sounds of distant waves crashing on a beach. It is the sound of the highway. We are approaching the town of Modeñedo and, like any big town, the only way to get to the center is to walk along the approach roads for a long, long time.

Mondeñedo

"Did you know," David begins. Uh oh! Here comes a teaching moment. I smile and listen. "There is a legend from Mondoñedo. It is about a woman who refuses to give bread to a needy pilgrim, who in turn, curses her. 'May your bread turn to stone.'

"When the woman goes to take the loaf out of her oven, she sees a large rock where her bread was. She repents and runs after the pilgrim, but he is nowhere to be seen," David tells me. Automatically, I look around for the distraught woman.

Does this mean that the people of Mondeñedo are mean and stingy, or just that pilgrims are vengeful?

My contemplation dissolves as car fumes overwhelm. We are now walking next to faceless warehouses imprisoned behind tall chain-link fencing. It is dismally gray.

Under the leaden sky, our hotel looks sad and abandoned. The staff are tired specters doing their daily chores. But the sight of David's backpack leaning against the bar injects happy into me. Correos really did deliver. Life gets even better when we discover the hotel not only has a self service washing machine, but a dryer too. This is very exciting, as with the humidity at 90%, we would be wearing wet socks and pants tomorrow. Today we can wash all our clothes.

The cold drabness demands hot chocolate or a hearty hot chicken soup, and a nice long soak in an Epsom salts bath. No soup on the menu. We order fish and chips, and then off we trot into town to look for the salts.

It is impossible to miss the imposing thirteenth century cathedral that dominates the main square. The guidebook says it is a mishmash of Romanesque, Gothic and Baroque archi-tectures, but to my untrained eye, it simply looks so old that it bleeds history and mystery. What is unusual is that instead of a saint crowning the church entrance, there is a giant statue of a bishop glaring down from his pedestal in the sky.

The notes say that the Episcopal palace, as the bishop's house is called, was added on to the cathedral at the same time the church was enlarged. I can only imagine the pomposity of the narcissistic bishop who used his power and the church purse to create this monstrosity that dominates the town and its main square. This is an eighteenth century Trump Tower.

"Why Episcopal palace? I thought that was the name of a Protestant Church," I ask.

"It just means it's the bishop's palace," David says. "The Episcopal church got its name because it was governed by the bishops, not the Pope in Rome."

He then he pulls up a random fact. "Do you know what Robin Williams said?" I didn't have to answer. "He said, being Episcopalian is great! It's like diet Catholic. . . All the religion of Catholicism, and only HALF the guilt!" Despite myself, I snort with laughter.

We chase around for Epsom salts. I have the translation and description all ready on Google to show pharmacists. "Go to the droggería," the pharmacist says. At the droggería, the drugstore attendant says, "Try the pharmacist."

As we pound the miles of Modeñedo's narrow streets, my foot complains violently. It's time for a glass of cold beer to chase down the Ibuprofen. At all the Spanish bars, they are more than happy to fill my Ziploc bag with ice. It has been a foot-saver. With my feet on ice, all is good until our next foray -- the search for places to dine that serve dinner before 9:00 pm and also have vegetables on the menu. We walk, reading menu after menu on the front doors of closed restaurants, until my foot screams "Just stop!" We end up at the nearest bar, which serves nothing but pizza before 8:30 pm. "The chef is still at home," the bartender says. Pizza it is.

Everywhere we look there is a television screen. On one, we watch a group of people running from one abandoned storage locker to another in a game show where the hosts auction the locker contents lock, stock and barrel. Will the contestant find some invaluable treasure buried amid the junk that is crammed inside? It's an American TV show called *Storage Wars*. The TVs are muted, thank goodness. It feels more exotic reading the subtitles in Spanish, instead of listening to the trash Hollywood spurts out to the rest of the world in English. "This show is really popular," says the bartender. Unbelievable!

Tomorrow we have an eleven mile uphill hike. I cannot wait to leave Modeñedo.

Day 4: On the trail to Abadín.

Home Sweet Camino.

Each morning my feet feel renewed. Each new day, hope wells up from my core that somehow, when I walk into the early morning mist, my feet will heal themselves.

The routine of preparing my feet, packing the pack for Correos to pick up, walking to our next albergue, and hand-washing the day's clothes is already as familiar and comforting to me as rubbing lotion on my body after a hot shower. Already we have the beginnings of a Camino family, wishing us *Buen Camino* as they pass by, and with whom we cross paths at cafés or at communal dinner tables. Sometimes we walk together for a little while just chatting. Sleeping around is not a problem -- by that I mean a different bed every night. I have come to see the actual Camino, the trail, and the routine as my home.

With memories of *Storage Wars* and the quest for Epsom salts and vegetables safely tucked away into my journal, we scurry across Mondeñedo while the town still sleeps. At the ancient well, just on the other side of the Cathedral, we pick up the Camino mile-marker. I make a mental note of the figures on the cement milestone with the blue and gold clam shell embossed into it. It notes the distance we still have to walk to Santiago de Compostela: 136 kilometers, it says. Ninety-seven miles!

Other pilgrims are converging in ones and twos, also scuttling out of town to hit the trail. We nod to each other, and before we know it, we are back in the countryside. The new morning belongs to us. The Rachael Carson quote I read this morning is my inspiration for today's walk:

"Those who dwell among the beauties and mysteries of the earth are never alone or weary of life."

Twelve miles with a 1600 foot rise, here I come. "Hi Mum!" Those familiar footfalls are right there with me. As I put one foot in front of the other, it hits me that millions before me have done exactly the same.

This is holy ground I'm stepping on.

I visualize a medieval young woman being fitted out for the Camino by her village. There is the poignant last supper with the family, where her mother gives the new pilgrim a loaf of bread, and with a heavy heart blesses the journey. While her face remains stoic, her heart whispers to the heavens, "Dear God, dear Santiago, watch out for my child. Grant her the redemption she seeks, and bring her home safely." A bishop anoints the pilgrim and gives her the *credencial* that announces her as a Peregrina de Santiago. Someone puts a mantle on her shoulder to keep off the rain. With a staff for walking, and a

gourd for drinking, she sets out without glancing back at her village. It's just her, her faith and the long road ahead.

As small stones and fallen twigs scrunch under my Vibram soles on the rutted, dung-strewn path, the picture of ancient pilgrims walking in thin, hand-sewn leather coverings that pass for shoes makes my feet recoil. Festering foot sores and plantar fasciitis must have plagued them. Fortunately, my lady pilgrim's *credencial* would have given her access to the network of missions and religious orders who sponsored inns and hospitals to care for the thousands of pilgrims that came through. Nowadays the Camino is mostly a one-way street, but back then not only did the pilgrims have to walk to Santiago, but then there was the return journey home, too. How different must it have been back then when bandits and hungry wolves roamed the land, waiting to pounce. No credit cards, no GPS, no mile markers and no Correos to pick up and deliver their possessions to the next inn.

Why would anyone want to undertake such a punishing pilgrimage? What sins had they committed? Maybe they were seeking a miracle, or maybe their faith drove them to venerate the relics of the saint as an act of worship. Maybe they had to prove to their God that they were worthy of His divine favors. Maybe this was the price they had to pay for absolution to avoid purgatory.

As I walk I am experiencing the same rhythm of foot-to-path that has marked every pilgrim in every time. I am forging the same bonds with fellow pilgrims. I am seeing the same mountains and crossing the same rivers.

I listen.

Do I hear echoes of the many voices that preceded me on the Way of St. James?

No, but I hear my dear husband's "Did you know . . ?" I am all ears. He is the best history teacher ever.

Did you know?

". . . That Santiago's bones weren't discovered until 800 years after he died? It was the hermit Pelayo who saw some mysterious lights in the woods of Lebredón, they say, and he told the local bishop about it. The bishop fasted and prayed, and then announced to King Alfonso of Asturias, that he had discovered the resting place of St. James. The king ordered a small church to be built over the tomb in 834. Word got around, and people naturally came to venerate the bones of this man who was an apostle and friend of Jesus. That was the beginning of the pilgrimage."

"But how did they even know that St. James came to Spain?" I ask.

"They really don't. All we know from the Bible is that he was martyred in 44 AD by Herod Agrippa, in Jerusalem. And the

Eastern Orthodox traditions don't mention Spain at all. They say that James preached in Judea and Samaria – yes, among the good Samaritans! – until his death. Never left the Holy Land.

"The Spanish Catholic tradition is totally different, of course. It says that James preached in Hispania around 40 AD, and then returned to Jerusalem to meet his fate at the hands of Herod. You remember the Slaughter of the Innocents in the Bible, where Herod killed all the boy children in Palestine to get at baby Jesus, and Mary had to run away to Egypt? That Herod was this guy's grampa. Charming family."

No, I don't remember. I must have been asleep during that history lesson, but then I have to ask, "If James died in Jerusalem, how did his body wind up here?"

"That's where it gets interesting. They say two disciples carried his body by sea back to Spain, in a boat made of stone, with no rudder or sails. It was guided by angels through the Pillars of Hercules and on to the stormy coast of Galicia. Then, after many adventures, the faithful disciples took the body inland, and buried it at the site that became Santiago de Compostela."

"Sounds like one hell of a funeral," I say.

"Doesn't it? Nobody knows exactly how the legend of James in Spain got started. There's nothing in the early Church documents, but there must have been an oral tradition, because we know that by the mid-700's several of the *Lives of the Saints* manuscripts were repeating the St. James story, including the bit about being buried in Galicia.

"So why would they make up stories about James in Spain?"

"Well, if you were a medieval Spaniard, wouldn't it make you hugely proud to think that less than ten years after Jesus died, his good friend James came to THIS country to spread the light of Christianity? No joke; the idea of a sacred center in the far West of Christendom was very powerful in the Middle Ages. It created a kind of divine balance between Santiago in the West, Jerusalem in the East, and Rome in the middle.

"And let's face it, saintly relics used to be a big deal for Catholics, and the discovery of James' bones was like winning the jackpot for the Christians in Iberia. In the 800's, three-quarters of Spain and Portugal was occupied by the Muslim Moors, and it was only the north coastal strip that was still in the hands of Christians. And by the grace of God, that's where James' remains were found.

"This happened a lot in medieval Europe – holy relics were miraculously discovered in more or less the same place where the legends said they would be. Relics lead to shrines, shrines attract pilgrims, pilgrims donate money. The shrine of Santiago attracted pilgrims from all over Christendom, and with them came money, roads, bridges and hospitals, new settlers, and a rallying-point to recruit forces for the re-conquest of Spain."

It takes me a while to absorb the fact that we are doing all this walking just to get to a made-up spiritual tourist trap. But then, David is quick to point out that the sacredness of the pilgrimage never did come from the bones. "They are just an excuse; the journey becomes holy to the extent that each pilgrim makes it holy. That is true of all pilgrimages, at all times. It's true for us.

". . And besides that," David continues, "The hermit was a true believer, and the bishop was well versed about the legend of St. James. So when he saw the bones in his own back yard, how could he not believe? This was a divine miracle. This is the power of faith."

"So who is REALLY in that tomb?" I ask my apostate husband.

"We don't know, but it probably isn't James. Archeologists say that the site at Lebredón, where the body was originally found in the ninth century, was a burial ground that had been used since Roman times, and at one time was next door to a Roman encampment. In fact, the word *Compostela* might come from *composita tella*, meaning 'burial mound'. My guess is that it's just some Roman, or Romanized local who is buried there."

"Really? I thought *Compostela* meant field of the star," I interrupt.

"Yeah, I know, *Campus Stellae* is way more romantic and cool than *burial mound*. But the linguists say that's not how it would have played out in medieval Galician."

And that is the gospel according to husband David.

I wish I had a recorder so that I can include this incredible piece of I-never-knew-history in my book, whenever I get down to writing it. I do the next best thing, which is to ask David, "Can you write down what you told me, exactly the way you said it, 'cause you know about my colander brain." He is quite amused.

"*Buen Camino!*" a couple of walkers call out. I don't even see them coming. They hustle past us. The backs of their packs recede, but I can still see the scallop shells swinging like pendulums with each step. "There's an interesting legend about how the scallop shell became the symbol for the Camino, but I'll save that for another day," David tells me.

I can't wait, just like the king in the Arabian nights' story who had to wait for the next episode to be told by his very clever queen.

Right now, I must ice my feet, sip my beer, eat my requisite ham and cheese boccadillo, and munch on a plateful of French fries.

Day 5: Abadín to O Xistral

Abadín becomes just a place to sleep, for I do not have an ounce of energy to pound the streets and discover the charms of the town. My first impression: it's a barren concrete place, suffering from a severe shortage of cobblestones. I'm happy just hanging out at the bar. What sheer luxury it is to just sit and admire the pictures I took today, check my e-mail and pore over the *Likes* and *hearts* and comments from friends on Facebook. Normally I am extremely critical of the *Likes* that litter Facebook, but right now I am delighting in all the people who are following my journey. Today I post, "I made it! My feet didn't fall off and I didn't need to be rescued. One hundred miles left to go. We are in Abadín."

One friend wrote "Only 100 miles! You can do it!! Keep those tootsies happy, and I know you'll get there! Wish I were there, pilgrimming along with you." Another wrote, "I hope your feet forgive you!" and yet another said, "You guys are tearing through!"

The next morning, instead of walking the next 15 miles to Vilalba, we choose to take a short five mile stroll to Castromaior, just so that we can stay in one of those lovingly restored 19th century wood and stone farmhouses. We also want to give my feet another day to pluck up.

Oh my, there are hammocks in the garden! I no longer care that it's nippy. How can I possibly pass up the opportunity of swinging in the lap of luxury? I last long enough for David to take my picture before I run in to warm my frozzled nose and toes. Our host has an array of teabags, trays of cookies and cakes, bowls of fresh fruit, and beer in the fridge -- and an honesty box to drop our Euros in. Tea and almond cake is what my inner doctor orders for today.

At the communal dinner, as we tuck into the lentil soup that our host has prepared for us, I ask the other pilgrims, "What drove you to walk hundreds of kilometers?"

"Because, for these three weeks, the worries of the everyday life, work, family and friends, conundrums, politics, all get left behind," says the Spaniard. Okay, he didn't actually say conundrums, I did.

"It is a cleaning of the mind," says Martha, the Austrian. She has just quit her job and is taking eight months off to decide what next. "What better way to start than to walk the Camino?" she asks. "But walking alone has been harder than I thought. I had to walk an extra 13 kilometers over and above the 20K to find a bed, because I was afraid to sleep on a park bench or on the beach."

The Italian says, "A cheap holiday. Don't have to plan. Can just go." She actually has very little time, so for this last part, she rented a bike. "Boy, that's turning out to be its own adventure. The poncho that was meant to keep me dry, filled out like a sail in the high wind, and tried to lift me and the bike into the sky." I think back to Casa Gloria in Mondeñedo, where Papa told us to avoid the mountain route because it was a meteorological disaster. Nobody told the Italian that, and she rode her bike straight up that mountain, where she had some definite Mary Poppins moments. "Very Scary!" she says, "But I am here."

Day 6: O Xistral to Vilalba

It is early morning, and a newborn baby horse is trying to find his feet as he reaches for mamma, who keeps moving further away -- just like a human mother moving back in the pool, urging her child to swim that extra stroke. I watch until the foal finds mama's nipple. My heart is bleeding love all over the place.

Pumpkins and squashes, pimientos and kale, and other leafy greens crowd the fenced in gardens. Are the greens for the animals, or people? I wonder. How I wish they would find their way onto my dinner plate. Zillions of rows of corn crisscross the countryside. Our flat 10-mile walk is accompanied by the occasional caw-caw of crows, the dull muted sound of bells around the necks of sheep, and the hum of traffic from the N634.

"Oh look, one farmer has set up a table." My eyes light up in delight. Fresh strawberries, plums, nectarines, hunks of cheese, and small rounds of fresh-baked bread for a couple of Euros -- and an honor basket to drop your money in. The nectarine is dribble-down-your-arms-to-the-elbows juicy. It is so sweet that I cannot help but lick my arm so as not to miss a single drop.

I need a potty break, but the next café is at least an hour away. I look for bushes to sneak behind and have a Ziplock bag ready to put my used tissues in. My chosen bush, it turns out, is everyone else's chosen pit stop too. It is littered with clumps of toilet tissue. Yuk! Yuk! Yuk! It's unbelievable. So superior am I for carrying my waste away. But then I wonder, what did medieval pilgrims do? I'm sure toilet paper and Sears catalogue pages didn't exist back then.

Toilet tissue aside, and despite the beautiful easy walk, my left hip and my right foot moan and groan. The Ibuprofen has had little effect. Maybe it is because this portion of the walk is on asphalt instead of sandy, gravely trails cushioned with fallen leaves and pine needles. I have no choice but to take loads of breaks and do the hokey pokey in slow motion to encourage my joints. *You put your right foot in* (Ouch!), *you put your right foot out . . ..*

We pass from farm country to the concrete, tarmac, and gray of parking lots, apartment buildings, and blocky warehouses. The delicate sound of footfalls without footprints is lost in the hiss and roar of the N634 into Vilalba, as is my heart's gentle chatter. Not a store or a restaurant is open, and there's hardly a soul on the street. It is 1:30 pm on a Saturday afternoon. The main door to our hotel is locked.

Oh no! My heart races and brain overheats as we peer through shut windows, to see chairs on the tables, and no sign of human beings. *So much for booking ahead and prepaying the room.* We walk around the corner to find all the patio furniture stacked. We try a door, it falls open. *Phew!* "Hola! Hola!" we call. The owner is rattling around behind a long bar, cluttered with racks of old and tired Twinkie-style junk food.

"Where is everyone? Is it siesta time for the whole town?" I ask.

"No, it is fiesta time at the river."

A fiesta. Aren't we lucky!

"You are not going to the fiesta?" I ask our matronly patron.

"Too much alcohol. I don't like it."

"Do you have any food?"

"No! Kitchen closed. Fiesta." The proprietor struggles with her English.

"Beer?"

"Si señora." She draws a couple of glasses.

What is better than eating two-day old, pre-packaged sliced ham and cheese sandwiches? Anything but that, but we don't have a choice. The beer makes it taste better. I push my tired old legs to climb the two flights of stairs and just flop into bed in this equally tired old box of a room. At this moment, laying my aching bones down is untold luxury. The laundry, the shower, they can all wait.

Several hours later, I soak in the shallow, narrow square tub, big enough for just half my body. For a while I prop my legs up on the wall, while the top half of me soaks. Bathtub yoga indeed.

With both my spirits and feet revived, we set out for the fiesta.

"It is one or two kilometers," one gent says, with an expression that tells us we must be mad to want to walk it. After 20 kilometers, what's another couple? Besides, I am newly energized. Down, down, down we walk around twisting narrow streets. Buildings are shuttered. We see a rambunctious group of people coming up. *They must be coming from the fiesta,* I think. We go where they came from. Music and noise make the air vibrate with the rhythm of a drumbeat. We must be getting closer. The streets shrink into a fan of alleyways, each of them a dead end. Yet we can see the jammed parking lot in the thick canopy of trees marking the river.

"How do we get there?" we finally ask the only other pedestrian we see. "Make a right and a right and a right." At least now no raised eyebrows at the crazy idea of walking there.

Bagpipes beckon. It is an isolated group of friends drinking beer and making music. We listen from afar. "That's the *gaita*, the Galician bagpipe." David tells me.

"Spanish bagpipes? You are laying on the blarney, aren't you?" David does have a missing Irish gene.

"Weeell," he says as we head down to the river walk and the fiesta. "At the time of the Romans, northwest Spain was full of Celtic-speaking tribes, and when you compare Galicia to rural parts of Ireland, there's still a whole lot of overlap in the DNA people are carrying around."

Here comes another did-you-know moment.

"In fact several people have told me they think of Galicia as one of the seven Celtic nations, along with Ireland, Scotland, Wales, Cornwall, Brittany, and the Isle of Man. In the 1980s, Galicia actually applied to be an official member of the Celtic League, but they got kicked out after a year or so because some of the other members protested on language grounds. Even though it's got a lot of Celtic words, modern Galician is kind of a cross between Spanish and Portuguese, and the purists said you can't have a Gaelic identity without the language. Anyway, even if it's just romantic make-believe, people here seem really proud of their Celtic side." He takes a deep breath to say more. I try to change the subject but he is on a roll. "I mean, there's only like 229 old people who actually speak Cornish, and they get to play. . . so why not Galicia?"

"I don't know dear. I didn't know that there were precisely 229 Cornish speaking folks, and why would you or anyone want to store a fact like that?" He gives me that I-cannot-help-it-if-I-am-so brilliant look.

"Did you just make that up?"

His father before him was a genius at making up statistics for anything he didn't want you to do, or have, or just to sound smart. "Can I have a motorbike, Dad?" would be met with, "Did you know that 64.2% of kids your age get serious brain injury from motorcycle accidents?" The extra decimal place is what gives the figure its credibility, of course. David has that same gene but he also truly knows a baffling amount of information.

After more than forty years of marriage, I still cannot tell the difference between brilliance and bullshit.

When we finally arrive at the festival the last thing we expect is to walk into a tent city. First, a cluster of one and two-man tents dot the grassy banks. Then bunches and bunches of larger party tents with zipped-up clear plastic walls press against each other. Humongous coolers are parked outside each of them. Boom-boxes are blasting, kids are running amok, and adults crowd picnic tables littered with empty wine and beer bottles. The entire riverside is one enormous tenement, or should I call it a tent-a-ment? This explains why the whole town is shuttered up, apartments, stores, cafes and all. They are all camping out here.

But where is the fiesta? There must be a stage or several stages, some center, the heartbeat of the festival?

We come upon a short row of stalls selling hippie tie-dye clothes and slinky beachwear. Plastic doodads dangle to attract the kids. The place is bursting with beer tents and pop-up bars, and the air crackles with alcohol-powered excitement and laughter. Bang in the middle of this bar area is a two-story, neon green, red and yellow kid's plastic air-filled adventure playground, complete with slides, tunnels and trampolines. There are no food stalls. We've been counting on eating here. I guess they must drink their dinners, for all we find is a tiny hot dog cart, and two vans serving burgers.

Hamburgers it is. The challenge now is to find somewhere to sit away from the loudspeakers. "Aha! There's a rocky crag we can perch on and people-watch while we eat," I say. We settle down, feeling somewhat pleased with ourselves that this primo spot had not already been claimed. From there, what do we find for our viewing pleasure?

A stream of men pissing against a wall behind large industrial size garbage tips, right next to the string of porta-potties.

As for the hamburgers, they elevate Big Macs to the level of a gourmet delicacy.

So this is the Fiesta. One drunken party for the whole town camped out for the weekend by the river.

We trudge back to our boxy room with its charming mural of a bridge spanning both beds. My feet are totally buggered from the extra 3 to 4 miles of pavement walking. On the way back, we search for more food in the still shuttered town. One tiny liquor store is open. The thought of drinking our supper is quite attractive at this point. Lucky us, they have cheese, crisps, pre-packaged cakes with super long shelf lives, and some fruit that looks ready to sprout baby trees. We pick up apples, cheese, ham and whole wheat melba toasts for tomorrow's thirteen mile walk to Baamonde . . . and beer for tonight.

Day 7: Vilalba to Baamonde

The owner of the hotel comes in especially to make us tea and coffee. She gives me a super sticky, chocolate covered, cream-filled cake left over from who-knows-what era. It is so filled with kindness and generosity, I have to say yes. Thank goodness I have 13 miles ahead to walk it off. I can't wait to leave town and get back in the country, smell the eucalyptus, listen to the river and see what the Camino has in store for us. As we walk the length of the town back to the river to pick up the Camino trail, not a soul stirs. Not a coffee bar open.

The early morning light clears our heads of extraneous thoughts and creates a pristine space. We delight in the glossy, jet black slugs that cross the road. The leaves rustle in the morning breeze and the sun glints off rows and rows of plastic-wrapped bales of hay. Cows and horses lazily munch and hang out, unbothered by the hordes of flies glued to their snouts. Farm wives in their ruffled aprons are already out feeding the barnyard animals.

I am in a state of quiet contemplation. I'm walking the Camino without any purpose, allowing space for serendipity. Just maybe I should walk for a cause. For every mile I walk I could pledge a

$10 donation to those who have walking ailments of the right foot. My mum would have relished the pain and suffering, as it burns away sins, and would have easily dedicated her journey to God.

The sight of a baby hanging by her neck from a branch jerks me out of my meditation. For all the world it looks like a real baby. It's a doll that is meant to scare the crows away, but still. What kind of person does that? A few yards further are a dozen cows in chains and yokes with tags stapled to their ears. Are they headed to the slaughterhouse? Am I in a Grimm fairytale? Will I be lured by innocence and curiosity to a witch's cauldron? Oh my!

I pick up my pace to get the hell out of this enchanted village. I find myself reciting, *Bubble, bubble, toil and trouble, fire burn and caldron bubble.* I used to recite this spell to torment my pesky kid brother before I even knew who Shakespeare was.

Further down the road, I catch sight of a heap of backpacks and the clutter of walking sticks leaning against an outer wall. It's a café. I am safe and among my scallop-shell-carrying Camino family.

"I wonder how the scallop shell became a symbol of St. James," I ask David as I sip my tea. David is engrossed in a phone app that tells us where to take our next potty break. But he loves these kinds of questions and readily puts the phone down.

"There is a popular legend about a wedding on the beach. The groom and guests were playing a game where they had to throw their lances in the air and then catch them on horseback before they hit the ground. When it was the groom's turn, a gust of wind deflected his lance out to sea. Determined to get it back, the young man rode out into the ocean and sank beneath the waves. When he didn't come back up, everybody assumed he had drowned. But just then a boat approached, and horse and rider both rose from the waters . . . covered in scallop shells! The boat was, of course, the renowned rudderless, sail-less stone boat that carried the remains of St. James from Palestine to Galicia. The Saint's own disciples, Atanasio and Teodoro, decided that, as a sign of devotion and in memory of this miracle, all who pilgrimage to the tomb of the Apostle Santiago should bring this symbolic shell."

"Wow, they traveled in a stone boat without sails from Palestine, through the Mediterranean and ploughed the stormy Atlantic to Galicia? From where do the Christians get their myths?" I asked rhetorically. But surprise, David has an answer.

"Nobody really knows. The Stone Boat story is a johnny-come-lately addition to the James legend. When they discovered James' tomb in the early 9th century, they had a problem, right? Everybody knew that James was martyred *in Jerusalem* by Herod Agrippa because it's right there in the Bible. So the storytellers had to find a way to get James from Spain -- where he was supposedly preaching -- to Jerusalem to get executed, and then BACK to Spain. And Lo, it came to pass. Within 30 years of the discovery of his Spanish tomb, collections of martyrs' tales were proclaiming that James' body had been returned to Spain and buried close to the British Sea. I have no idea how the details of the stone boat got cobbled together, but it must date to at least the mid 9th century." With a chuckle he added, "Isn't it interesting that they even knew the names of the two disciples who brought the remains over."

Sounds like medieval priests and popes have a lot in common with some present day politicians who are in the business of creating alternate truths. Were they also stable geniuses? Biblical myths, politicians and Grimms' stories run in parallel universes. I'm walking in one, being tormented by the other and conjuring up the last concurrently.

I muse in silence. These are such outrageous stories -- a stone boat, without sails, guided by angels and an apparition of the Virgin that appears to order James back to Jerusalem to be slaughtered. People really believed and still believe these stories. Incredible!

Then I think of today's information-rich world where facts are just a click away, and yet many believe so many things that are blatantly untrue. This wanting to believe and repeating lies so often that they become true is as old as humanity.

It occurs to me that even I do it. I have this story about the footfalls I hear every morning as I set out to walk. I maintain the delusion that my long dead mum is walking with me. It comforts me. It brings magic into my world. It lifts me into a spiritual realm. As I repeat this story over and over, I am seriously beginning to believe that my mum is really walking with me on the Camino. It does indeed make for a richer world. I wonder what other delusions I'm turning into realities? What alternate Universes am I creating that allow me to accept lies? Plenty to meditate on for the rest of the walk!

Baamonde

We are half-way. Hurray! One hundred and one more kilometers (about 63 miles) to go.

We stop at Bar 101 to celebrate, but it is jam-packed with hot and weary faces like ours, mixed in with fresh, rosy-cheeked ones. For the latter, this is the beginning of their Camino.

Baamonde is just outside the 100 kilometer circle that you have to walk, at minimum, to qualify for the *Compostela* -- the fancy certificate saying that you did the pilgrimage. According to the Pilgrim's Office, to get the *Compostela:*

- You must make the pilgrimage for religious or spiritual reasons, or at least with an attitude of search.

- You must, at a minimum, do the final 100 km entirely on foot or horseback, or the final 200 km if cycling.

- You must collect the stamps on the Credencial del Peregrino from the places you pass through to certify that you have been there. Stamps from churches, hostels, monasteries, cathedrals and all places related to the Way are preferred, but if not, they can also be stamped at other institutions: town halls, cafés, etc. During the last 100 kilometers (foot or horseback) or the last 200 (cyclists), the credencial must be stamped at least twice a day until you reach the tomb of St. James.

I am too tired, cranky and hungry -- a lethal combination, as my husband will tell you -- to hang out with other pilgrims. Instead, we walk on to look for a quieter café where we can have a table and be waited on. We have a couple of hours to squander before our pre-arranged ride comes to take us to the hotel.

As a special treat, David has booked two nights at a luxurious *hotel rural*, the Bi Terra, where we can take a break from our walking, have all our clothes washed, fluffed and folded by someone other than us, as well as have a celebratory dinner in their fancy dining room.

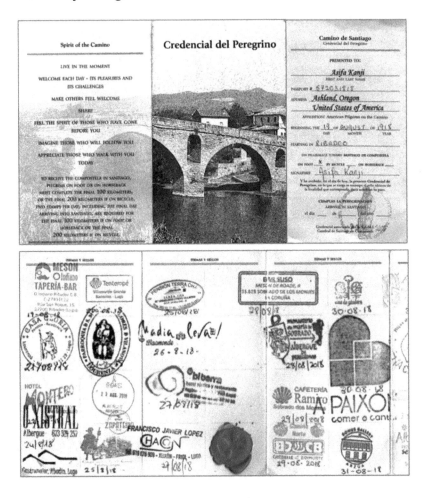

When David asked, "Would you like to spend a couple of days off the trail in a gorgeous off the beaten track hotel?" I did not even blink. "Yes please. Do they have a spa?" A vision of my naked body laid out on a massage table, under an oh-so-soft towel, in a candle-lit, fragrant room delighted my mind.

"It's not that fancy. But, they will pick us up in Baamonde and drop us further down the trail when we leave. It will cut several miles from our walking. This is important because the longest walk without any place to stay is from Baamonde to Sobrado -- some 25 miles, which is our next stretch," he says.

We have yet to take short cuts, but torturing my feet with a 25-mile walk gives fear a large megaphone. Amputation? Permanently disabled? *Just this once,* I think. But my conscience prods me, *You are a cheat.* Fear quashes the little voice.

When we run our plan by our host, Javier, he insists, "You must do the walk between Baamonde and Seixon. That is the most beautiful part of the trail. Do that tomorrow. Then I will take you directly to Sobrado on the following day. You will miss nothing, as the walk from here to Sobrado is boring and dangerous. It is all on main the road with very fast moving traffic."

"What! Walk tomorrow on my day off?" I say, while David is tap tapping into his app to find just how long the walk between Baamonde and Seixon is. "It's only eight miles, and since we are coming back to our hotel, you don't have to carry anything on your back." That's appealing.

Day 8: Baamonde to Seixon

Javier drops us off at the trailhead in Baamonde. "Call me when you arrive in Seixon. I'll pick you up."

Our walk follows a stream in the wild forest. For the first time ever since we began, we hear a sonata of birdsong. I linger to listen and cock my head this way and that to see if I can spot members of the chorus.

"There are almost no birds or insects left in Spain," a passerby tells us. "Too many decades of chemical fertilizers has killed all the worms and insects. This forest is an oasis. Enjoy!"

Ouch!

I've wondered why none of the places we have stayed have screens on the windows or doors. Even the mosquitoes and gnats can't make a living here. I wish it were also true for the pesky flies. There are always a couple that get into our room, torment us, and force us to perform ungainly fly-swatting pirouettes as we chase them.

You were right, Javier, I would have hated to miss this part of the walk. We go from forest to rolling hills sculpted by farmers over many centuries. But the neatly cultivated rows of pastoral beauty make my heart and soul cry for the soil that is too dead to support worms and bugs. How can any landscape so sterile look so bountiful and beautiful? No more birdsong, just the caw-caw of black crows and the buzz-buzz of flies.

As we enter a hamlet, I see snakes. They are carved into the stone walls that fence a house. After the hanging baby-doll experience, I am leery but curious. The tall pillars of the archway around the gate are hand-engraved with decorative curvy spirals. A faded framed picture of an old man with an obituary below, hangs on one side of the gate. Dusty plastic flowers stick up from behind the frame. I poke my nose into the front yard. It's a museum of intricate stone carvings that could have been lifted from ancient Indian temples. The house is all shuttered up. We dare to let ourselves into the garden. No sooner do we do that, an apparition appears at the doorway. Oh no, we have been caught trespassing. An old man, whose bony frame shows signs of crumbling, shuffles out.

"Would you like a stamp?" he asks. Before we can answer, he is already lifting his roll-top workshop door. I'm tongue-tied and gawk. I want to say, *If it is not too much trouble*, but I don't know how to say that in Spanish, so I say, "Si, por favor."

His studio is an artist's jumble, the walls randomly plastered with fading family photos, pictures of saints, and well-worn magazine pages. Maybe there is an order to the madness of his tools strewn over the heavy wooden tables. He lights a gas jet. What is he going to do? I search for answers on the nearby small table piled with little rectangles of red wax to seal important documents, stamps, quartzite-like rocks, and a bowl full of coins. He picks up a solid piece of wax and puts the flame to it so that the blood-red droplets fall onto my pilgrim's passport, creating a small puddle. He weighs down my booklet with the quartzite stones and then presses a metal stamp onto the wax. A Maltese cross? A four-leaf clover? It's hard to discern, but the hand-made stamp is delightful. I throw a few

Euros into his coin collection and accept his blessing. With our most treasured stamp yet, we walk on.

We find a big old laden apple tree to picnic under. It even has a bench to sit on. There we enjoy our sandwiches, scrounged from the hotel's breakfast buffet. Yes, it is ham and cheese, but also tomatoes and cucumbers.

"Eat me. Eat me!" A big fat green apple, dangling right above me, begs. I look for the serpent. Is this going to be a life-changing bite into the piece of stolen fruit? The tartness of the juice makes my whole mouth pucker. "It would make wonderful applesauce," I say as I toss the rest into a thicket.

It doesn't take long to walk the eight miles, despite our dawdling. It is just after noon and already we are in Seixon. We order cold beer at the bar while we wait for Javier to pick us up. Back at the hotel, he shows us his raspberry patch. "Please help yourselves," he says.

A nap and a shower -- what simple pleasures. With just one change of clothes, I don't even have to think about what to wear. After a leisurely gourmet dinner, I check out a map of the area as I finish the remnants of my wine. If we walk directly from the hotel, it's only 15 kilometers to Sobrado, which means we will have walked the whole way. Just the same, Javier's offer to drop us off in Sobrado and take the day off from walking is tempting.

Just because you are a credit card-toting pilgrim savoring every bite of big fat langoustines soaked in garlic and cognac followed by chocolate mousse doesn't mean you can take shortcuts, says the voice of my conscience. *Besides, who knows what you will miss?* she adds.

Day 9: Baamonde to Sobrado

Morning comes. Dark clouds hover. The wind bustles. It chills my bones.

It has rained already, but the ominous skies threaten to burst anew. The watery sunshine is losing ground, but look, there's a rainbow. As I hasten to the garden wall to frame a better picture, two ripe raspberries wink at me. They are delicious. Raspberries and rainbows, what more can I ask for? Oh yes, a decision on whether to walk or to catch a ride to Sobrado.

The thought of wading through muddy paths up a long slope before slipping and sliding down another one in the rain is hardly inviting. But encouraged by the rainbow and the raspberries, I still want to walk. "How about we skip the first ten kilometers and walk the last ten?" I suggest. Javier shrugs and drops us off on the road, half way to Sobrado. I know he thinks we are crazy to walk on such a horrible road in the rain.

It is indeed a busy curvy road with absolutely no shoulder. It is pouring, a cold, cold rain. We are breathing car fumes while avoiding backing into the blackberry thorns when cars whizz too close. *Hey that's a part of the experience*, I try to convince myself. Squelch, squelch go my un-waterproof shoes. Darn it, I should have packed a dry pair of socks in my daypack. Oh well. I start channeling hot chocolate.

Praise St. James, or somebody, for I see a hand-made cardboard sign stuck on a pole with a black arrow. It says "Café 300 meters". Yes, they do have steamy, hot chocolate. Somewhere in my youth or childhood, I must have done something good.

A mother-daughter duo are sipping coffee. Their feet are bare. Their socks are drying atop a pair of backpacks from which scallop shells dangle. "We are the two Tinas, Martina and Kristina," Mom says. She is 55, and Kristina is 25. From their accents, I guess they are German.

Mom tells us, "I have spent my life raising children, taking care of my grandparents, and now my parents. I give, but my spirit is empty. A couple of years ago, a neighbor who walks caminos all the time mentioned he was going to do a very short one, 'Take me with you,' I begged, and he did. We walked 25 kilometers (about 15 miles) a day, every day. I felt so liberated. For the first time in my whole life, I began to think about me. For the first time I set boundaries to protect myself. After seeing just how easy it was to walk the Camino, this year I decided to walk this one."

As for young Tina, she says "I was dying in my job, and my boyfriend . . . well, that is over now. I asked my mother if walking the Camino would help me find myself. I wanted time to think. I wanted to walk alone." And so she did for the first two weeks, before Mom joined her.

So how was that for you? I ask.

"I never felt so alone. Hardly anybody spoke German or English. They were all Spanish-speaking," she says. "But I did it, and now I know I can do anything. All I need is just my backpack, my shoes and me. I don't need a TV, clothes and all that stuff. I feel so free."

Tina and her Mom are walking together for the last two weeks of The Way. They are just three days from finishing. They both say that they love walking together. "We have become best friends."

I tell them the story of my mom walking with me. Up until yesterday, I suspected that the footfalls I was hearing were sounds my pack made. But I liked the idea that my mum was walking with me, so I didn't try to disillusion myself. However, yesterday I walked pack free, and within minutes of setting foot on the trail, those soft footfalls were right there with me. So it has to be her spirit caring for and hugging me. I really want to believe that. In life, we never walked together, let alone hugged each other. I never got to say *I love you mum*. Seeing this mother-daughter duet touched my core.

* * * * *

Like castles in the sky, the distant spires of Sobrado Abbey are a golden sight for tired eyes. They breathe a new energy into our walk on the tedious tarmac. But like a mirage they disappear and then reappear as we turn the next corner. Now they are looming large on the horizon. *We are almost there*, I think. I am so sure that the next bend will land us at its doorstep, but no. I swear those spires are walking away from me.

I'm so focused on the disappearing towers that I almost step on a frog. We have stumbled onto the shores of a lake created 500 years ago by the Cistercian monks. They stocked it with fish, the info board tells us. Today, it is a natural lake with its own ecosystem, complete with frogs, lilies, fish, birds and ducks -- and there are even some beavers.

"We have to keep moving," David nudges me. "Sorry my dear, but we have to be in Sobrado by noon. Remember the monastery shuts down between noon and 5 pm."

The view from the next curve makes my head spin and my jaw drop. Standing right in front of us is an absolutely massive, imposing medieval structure, the Monasterio Santa Maria de Sobrado dos Monxes. What man sacrifices and achieves in the name of God! One more corner to turn and we are there. We are actually going to spend the night in a monastery! I am so excited.

We step into this grand edifice. Its outer stones are heavily carved in intricate patterns that radiate a lacelike beauty. In stark contrast, the inside has been stripped of all the grandiose Catholic ornamentation -- no altar, no paintings of saints, no stained glass, no organ, no nothing -- just bare stone walls, standing silently, housing a couple of unmarked tombs with stone effigies lying on them. Moss creates living murals. Ivy creeps in from the outside to drape the broken windows and dangle down the interior walls. A lone dark skinny cross with Jesus hangs on the wall behind where the altar would have been, with a solitary candle burning. Raw beauty. Cold desolation.

Just like the pilgrim who is totally disconnected from worldly goods, carrying just one change of clothes and some bread and water for the journey, this church is totally disconnected from the ostentations of Catholicism.

I feel the love and sacrifice of thousands upon thousands of stonemasons and stone carvers who created this home for the Almighty.

I feel a strong sense of wonder, the same kind as when I lie on my back and stare at the stars, feeling the immensity of our Universe.

All the voices inside of me are silent.

Gratitude overcomes me, moves me to tears.

Gratitude for my life, for the beauty of the rainbow, for the raspberries, and for the creation of humankind.

Silently I stand and marvel, until the rumbles of hunger wake me up.

The main square in front of the Monastery is filled with tables shaded by umbrellas. It is the place to be to enjoy beer, platefuls of *pimiento padrónes* (locally grown green peppers, fried and served with olive oil and coarse ground salt. They are mild, except when they are not!), *boquerones* (mild white anchovies) and other Galician specialties. While waiting for lunch, I wonder out aloud what happened to all the church's treasures here in Sobrado.

"Look it up," says David.

"What you mean is you don't know," I tease.

"There must be two or three things I don't know,' he replies with utmost modesty.

When David fails me, Wikipedia is my backup.

The abbey was founded by a wealthy landowner, Count Hermenegildo in 952. It went through periods of flourishing and declining as ownership changed. To cut a long story short, eventually the Cistercians built this monumental new Baroque Abbey in the 17th century. But the glory and wealth of the Church was eyed by Prime Minister Mendizabal in 1835. He passed laws to dissolve and take over monasteries and Church property all over Spain, with the intention of redistributing the land to create a middle class. Surprise, surprise. It was the wealthy and the nobility who took advantage of the legislation to increase their holdings. During this time Sobrado was among countless monasteries and churches that fell into disuse and decay. Eventually some of the holdings were returned. It was as late as 1954 that the Cistercian monks began reconstruction and were able to resettle the monastery with a new community in 1966.

A private room in the Monastery is not cheap. Our room is hardly a monk's cell, which is what David and I were hoping for -- one whose ancient, bare stone walls imbue a sense of holy sacrifice and simplicity of thought. Instead, we are shown to a simple, climate controlled and functional room with a small prefab bathroom. Except for a cross above the bed, it is unadorned. The window overlooks an unkempt but still inviting garden. It is when we step out into the vaulted hallways that I sense the austerity and the history of this hallowed space.

With lunch done, we join a group of young pilgrims lounging around on the grass waiting for 5 pm, which is when we are allowed back into our accommodations.

"Why are you doing this Camino?" I ask the kids.

"It's about unplugging for a while," says one.

"You mean you left your smart phone behind as well?"

There is laughter all around as they realize they are still quite plugged in. In fact one guy says that because there is so little to do, he is on his phone even more. "Mostly I walk to meet the girls," he adds.

We drift away and find a shady spot to just be, except that I can't. Like the kids, I pull out my phone and begin googling. The Monastery's web site says:

The goal of our guest house is to receive all who are in search of an adequate place for personal reflection, a spiritual retreat or a peaceful and calm rest. Let all guests who arrive be received like Christ, for He is going to say, "I came as a guest, and you received ME."

Day 10: Sobrado to Boimorto

In Sobrado, what do we get for a €2.50 Euro pilgrim's breakfast?

A shot glass of orange juice, a giant croissant and a café grande con leche, all served by a surly waitress who really doesn't want to be here. I ask her what today's date is for the stamp in my pilgrim passport.

I wilt under her stare for daring to ask. "August 29. I should know, it's my birthday." Spontaneously, David and I burst into "Happy Birthday to you . . .," and clear our table for her. She smiles.

After breakfast, we return to our room to do the final packing and tie-down. We add our pack to the pile of already assembled luggage for Correos and head for the front door. It is padlocked! Where have all the monks gone? We are now trapped. "Hola! Hola!" Our voices bounce around the quiet courtyard. We try to return to our room, where we had done as we were told, leaving our keys behind in the room door. The access door to that wing is firmly locked too.

It is 9 am. We run around looking for any sign of humanity. Nobody. After an eternity, a middle-aged gentleman appears and looks at us very suspiciously, chides us for leaving our keys behind. Just had to take his scolding for neither of us had enough Spanish to explain. "Lo siento, I'm sorry." We are just dumb American pilgrims who didn't know we had to be out by 8 am. Fortunately we are not in a hurry, because it is a short walking-day to Boimorto.

Walking with the butterflies.

Leaving the monastery, silence and grace accompany us as we walk along the Avenue of the Oaks. Soon we cross the stone bridge onto a more open path. No sound of footfalls this morning. "Mum where are you? I miss you." No answer.

Orange and black butterflies are playing among the flowery, weedy verge. I stand still. At that very moment one of the flutterers rises up and flies in circles around me.

"David, David, a butterfly just flew around and around me." I cannot stop smiling. "It's my dad," I say.

Twenty-eight years ago, I had the same experience. It happened in the California Redwoods where I was hiking. My dad had just passed away. Our last walk together had been in the very same park. How he had loved it. The memory created a wave of grief that had me sobbing, "Daddy, please come back." Just at that moment a butterfly appeared from nowhere and circled me.

That very same smile from deep within hugged me. He was with me in spirit.

Here I am now with that same small voice asking, "Daddy, is that you?"

The butterfly flew ahead of me and perched itself on a blade of grass. A few moments later, when my shadow passed over him, he took off ahead of me and the same thing repeated itself over and over. David was right there with me watching this. We had never seen anything like it. That butterfly stayed with us all the way through the woods.

Is today's butterfly encounter my dad, or my mum or both? Truly, anything is possible on the Camino.

Day 11: Boimorto to Arzúa

Both my feet and spirits are soaring. Do they know that this is our last 10 kilometers on the Camino del Norte? Or are they euphoric because I'm eating avocado on toast for breakfast, instead of the usual sticky buns and sweet cakes? Whatever it is, I can't wait to step out and inhale that first breath of chilly air, the last remnant of the night.

Once on the trail, the bad news is that the waves of pilgrim traffic have increased since Sobrado. The good news is that the rush of hikers pushes right on past us, and the calls of *Buen Camino!* disappear quickly into the road ahead, leaving the countryside to us. We savor this last piece of quiet, watching farmers plow and bale hay, while fat cows take it easy and horses graze. Acres of corn stalks sway in the wind. Pungent chemical fertilizers twist our noses. Wafts of eucalyptus relax them. It's a quiet morning in the Galician countryside. We amble. Somewhere deep down, I don't want our Camino to end, so when I see a well-weathered wooden sign "Tavern on the river, 300 meters," I say to David, "Shall we?"

The café doesn't open for another half hour, but that doesn't stop us from making ourselves comfortable. From the maps and what we have read, Arzúa is not only the last major town before Santiago, but it is also the confluence of a couple of the smaller caminos -- del Norte and el Primitivo -- with the more popular and famous Camino Francés. Needless to say, we are not in a hurry to join Arzúa's helter-skelter of pilgrims in the home stretch. We sit by the stream and write in our journals under the shade of birches shimmering and quivering above us. The gentle breeze creates a dance of shadows.

I write in my journal:

It was never a pilgrimage for me, nor did I really want to do the Camino. It is the in thing. It's what others do, not I. I would have much rather gone to Mongolia and camp out in the Gobi Desert. I didn't force myself to walk the full 500 miles from Irun. I didn't take a chance on finding a bed, and I didn't carry my luggage. My limits were not pushed, and the adventure that is born of that did not happen. Yet I am surprised at how much I look forward each morning to start walking. I am surprised by the magic. More than anything, I love walking with the soft footfalls of my mum as company.

I throw a branch into the river and watch it get carried away by the current. That's me being carried by the flow. I ponder why, on a pilgrimage walk, all the churches are locked, but all the cemeteries are open. I ponder the lack of insects, despite the amount of dung on the trails. I marvel at the tiny Ibuprofen pills' ability to dissolve my pain.

The café's chef assembles a fresh omelet sandwich filled with lettuce, finely sliced carrots, onions and the requisite amount of ham, plus a nice cup of choice Earl Grey tea. For the moment I am a happy epicure. With the food eaten we must dally no longer, for the sun has moved quickly from defrost to bake.

Call for a taxi, my brain urges as we approach Arzúa. It's so tempting to do just that, as urban ugly assaults us -- tall, flat-faced cement block buildings, wide roads, traffic, fenced-in parking lots. Been there, done that. But nooo, even I, lover of ease and comfort, have some sense of shame. I put one foot in front of the other as fast as I can for what's left of the day's walk.

In search of our hotel pensíon, we step away from the main road and get lost in a maze of alleyways with absolutely charming old style rehabbed buildings. This is an Old Town that has become the new town, where cafés pour out onto the sidewalks and albergues, pensíones, and bargain accommodations announce their nightly rates on hand-painted blackboards. Beer and pizza joints abound. The town is geared for the low-budget pilgrim. The smell of French fries frying, seasoned with car exhaust, is everywhere.

Kids with backpacks, footsore, are finding their beds for the night. Some are reconnecting with their Camino families. We find a bar with a beautiful view of the hills and countryside, and order plates of *pimiento padrónes*, calamari, and a big mixed salad. Recipe for Spanish salad: take a whole can of tuna, dump it on a bed of iceberg lettuce, and sprinkle it with tomato, onion and ham. I still don't get what Spaniards have against vegetables. Why is there no cauliflower, broccoli, greens or any other summer vegetable? All main dishes always and only come with fried potatoes. Even the produce sections of grocery stores are tiny. David suggests that the only leafy green Spaniards consume is tobacco! Everyone smokes. In fact, we have seen many an empty cigarette box and butts ground into the Way of St. James.

At the grocery store, I retch at the sight of the hectares of shelf space dedicated to pork and ham cured every which way. As one fellow pilgrim put it, "In Spain, ham is a condiment." They sprinkle it on everything. I desperately want a break from ham and cheese, which has become a lunchtime staple for us. I search the shelves of this big city supermarket for anything different for tomorrow's lunch.

Bingo! Smoked salmon, and look, there are avocados in the veggie section! Praise be to Santiago. We buy extras.

Arzúa has its own bread and pilgrim story. Just as in Monteñedo, a baker refuses the young pilgrim's request for bread in exchange for prayers in front of the Apostle's tomb. So the pilgrim stops at the next bakery. This owner invites him in to rest a while. The pilgrim tells her he cannot stop, and that he only needs some food to recover his energy and keep walking. The lady is terribly distressed, as the bread she is baking is not quite ready. "If you are in a hurry, then all I can give you is yesterday's bread." She goes to fetch it, but on her return the young pilgrim is nowhere to be seen. When the lady opens the oven to pull out the fresh batch of bread, to her astonishment the bread has been transformed into gold! The opposite happens at the shop that turned him away. In that house, when they go to take the bread out, they find the oven full of stones. The Faithful nod knowingly; surely this was Santiago himself who had donned the guise of a humble pilgrim.

I am tempted to walk into a bakery and see if they will give me bread in exchange for prayers. But what if the spirit of St James -- the mean one -- knows I'm making fun of the miracle, and turns my smoked salmon into ham sandwiches? Such thoughts make me laugh at my own silliness and superstition.

Day 12: Arzúa to Salceda

Today the morning is different. It is as though we woke up at Grand Central Station in the midst of morning rush hour. The cafes are packed, as are all the little streets of Arzúa near the Camino. Pilgrims with their backpacks and walking sticks trickle out of their albergues like rivulets after a rain, to join the fast-flowing main stream, heading for the final destination. Just 39 kilometers, about 24 miles to go -- an eight hour walk.

For a thousand years, the great mother Camino, the Francés -- the veritable autopista, motorway, autobahn of Caminos -- has been the most famous route of Catholic pilgrimage, going from St. Jean Pied de Port over the Pyrenees to Santiago de Compostella.

"Starting in the eleventh century," David tells me, "The Francés became a superhighway for knights, settlers, builders, and also for French monks bent on purging the Spanish Christians of their deviant rites and imposing the Roman liturgy."

Deviant? My imagination immediately supplies a film roll of orgies, lounging and carousing at churches. "So were they being kinky?" I ask.

"Worse than that, from the Church's point of view. Many of the Spanish living under Moorish rule were taught to believe that God just kind of adopted Jesus, who began life as a mortal man. For the Roman Christians, that was plain straight heresy. The Cistercians, the forefathers of the monks at Sobrado, made it their business to straighten out the barbaric Spaniards."

As we join the caravan of pilgrims, I smell the incense at the Church in Santiago like a horse smells the barn. Part of me wants to push to walk faster and further and reach that coveted end, just like the others. Yet I hesitate. I am not ready for this journey to end. It's hard to believe that it was only two weeks ago we left home, and we've only been walking for 11 days -- Galicia in slo-mo. How many people have come in and out of our lives? The rolling green hills, the magical misty mornings, the lazy cows, handsome horses, bucolic little hamlets, female farmers in frilly gingham aprons, paunchy old men playing cards, and endless ham and cheese lunches -- all this has come to feel like home.

On today's walk, we are jerked into a different reality. Again and again, knots and clots of walkers overtake and swamp us in bursts. This stretch is a part of the final 100 kilometers on the Camino Francés, which is crowded by those who want the *Compostela* without walking too far. It is also immensely popular because it's on the route Martin Sheen traveled in the movie *The Way* – an inspiring story in which Martin Sheen's character Tom, an American doctor, walks the Camino to honor his son, finding an adventure of his own with a profound impact.

At first we stop to let the groups walk past, but soon realize that there will always be people behind us, people in front, and people passing on both sides. Moments of quiet, long enough to inhale and exhale and take in the scenery, become more precious. I no longer hear the soft footfalls walking next to me. Couples and groups walking with music blasting from their ipods and phones. People talking on the phone while calling out *Buen Camino!* to all they pass by. Singing groups. Lovers chasing each other, giggling, teasing. Bustling bars and cafes now punctuate the trail at a heady frequency. A tandem bike powered by papa and kid toots by us. Papa is doing most of the work. Loads and loads of groups. A few loners. Clickety clack, clack, clickety clickety clack, go the syncopated beats of walking sticks on the stony path. It feels like I've joined a party, but I don't know anybody there.

To spice up the circus, vendor stalls intrude onto the path. All the hand-painted scallop shells, scallop shell earrings, belts, watch straps, wallets and hand-carved walking sticks you could ever wish for. A song circle at one of the bars is singing *Country roads, take me home, to the place I belong . . .* It's a walking carnival infused with the smell of fertilizer, both organic and chemical, emanating from the rolling hills covered with cornfields and cow pastures. The path itself is actually a beautiful dirt trail lined with ivy-laden oaks, but it has lost its sense of innocence. The graffiti-covered kilometer stone markers distract, as do the rambunctious groups, for whom this is more a party than a pilgrimage.

We come upon a tree trunk whose base is cluttered with memorial cards, photographs and sentiments scribbled on pieces of paper. It arouses in me a morbid fascination about how the dead are remembered, or want to be remembered. I want to pick up and read some of the notes and cards. Would that be the equivalent of disturbing a tomb? I wonder why *this* tree, and whether all these people had died walking the Camino.

Just then a man shows up and stands beside me. He pulls out two holy cards from his breast pocket and holds them between the palms of his hands, praying silently. I see his lips moving. He kisses the cards and lays them down like one would a wreath at a tombstone. He then tucks a small piece of paper under a stone. When I try to offer my condolences, he tells me that on this pilgrimage he is praying for the living and the dead. He puts on his hat and walks on.

When I tell David this, he says this is a Catholic custom stemming from the Spiritual Works of Mercy.

"And what's that?" I have to ask.

"Let me see if I can remember. The nuns used to make us memorize all this in elementary school. He counts off on his fingers as he recites: "To instruct the ignorant . . . to counsel the doubtful . . . to admonish the sinner . . . to bear wrongs patiently . . . to forgive offenses willingly . . . to comfort the afflicted. . . oh yeah . . . and to pray for the living and the dead."

He reels these off like I would have my multiplication tables and smiles that proud-of-himself smile. "Sister Gemilla would give 10 gold stars for that."

I think of the religious man I just met. This is a spiritual journey for him, a time to be alone with God regardless of how much of a zoo this portion of the Camino is. In contrast, I'm such a tourist. This tree that acts like a community tombstone is just an interesting photo to take. But the man's offering makes me reflect a little. I contemplate the meaning behind all the sentiments and objects left here. I think of the people who walk the Camino because they have lost someone near and dear to them, as Martin Sheen did in the movie. I think of the people I've met who were walking to find new meaning and purpose for their lives. They all add to the conscious energy that flows on this path.

I tread more carefully now, respecting how sacred this journey is for some, and feeling blessed that I get to walk in the wake of their prayers.

Salceda

After just seven miles on the autobahn Francés, we leave the trail at Salceda to reclaim some peace and quiet and smell the hay. For almost all pilgrims, this is just a pass-through place. There are only two small roadside inns, and one of them, with the homely name of Aunt Teresa's, has a bar that serves breakfast and dinner. The mustachioed owner brings me an extra helping of the home baked Torta de Santiago, the cake of St. James, a Galician specialty and Camino staple made from almond flour, eggs, sugar, lemon rind and juice. The top of the cake is decorated with powdered sugar, crowned by an imprint of the Cross of Saint James which gives the pastry its name. "Don't share it with your husband. This is just for you," he winks at me. I can't say I flirt back, but I take quiet pleasure in the attention I am receiving.

Lucia, the only other pilgrim there, looks like a person who gets in her car to buy a liter of milk from the corner store, the kind of person who, every New Year's Eve, makes a resolution to lose weight and exercise more. "Why are you walking the Camino?" I ask, to strike up a conversation. She says she is from Italy. She is not religious, but she had made a vow that if her mom survived cancer she would walk the Camino. God took her up on the bargain. So here she is, totally unfit and unprepared for the journey. "My blisters burst and got infected. I couldn't walk for many days. The pharmacist gave me antibiotics," she says. "Now I am walking again." She smiles from ear to ear. "I know I'll get my *Compostela*."

Her feet are wrapped in bandages, and with a belly full of Paracetamol she conquers the Camino one slow step at a time. I thought I was being foolish walking with my fasciitis screaming at me. I worry about her. Will she cripple herself for life in exchange for her mother's recovery? If I were a praying person I would pray for her, but instead I offer her up to my mother. "Dear Mum, please walk with her and keep her safe."

Day 13: Salceda to O Podrouzo

At breakfast, Mr. Winking Bartender turns into a coffee cup artist. He draws silly faces on the foam of David's cappuccino.

He cuts a slice of the Torta de Santiago and gives me a small plate with two blackberry muffins.

Lucia looks like a homeless waif, with shells, shoes, and wet socks dangling from the straps of her backpack, which bulges like an oversized woman squeezed into an undersized cocktail dress. In one hand she grips a plastic grocery bag filled with bananas, and in the other a water bottle. She smiles a happy good morning and wishes us a *Buen Camino*. "Would you like to walk with us?" I offer. She waves me on. "Don't worry, I will be fine. I walk slowly, and my feet are doing better. I am only walking to Podrouzo," she says. I so badly want to believe her.

The great thing about starting in Salceda is, we have the Camino to ourselves. The walkers from Arzúa have yet to reach this portion of the trail. Blissfully we walk through the aisles of a cathedral of eucalyptus. Ten minutes later, the trail spits us out onto the roadside. We follow that for a while and then it meanders back into the woods and again out onto the open road with elevated highways crossing over us. As we enter the graffiti covered tunnel to Santa Maria, I sing, "Laaaaaah!" A sonorous echo bounces back at me.

David breaks out into *Ubi caritas*, an ancient chant that says, *Where charity and love are, God is there also*. The acoustics are so great that my very own Pavarotti pulls out his phone to record an encore performance in the tunnel to Santa Maria.

I spy a dead rat, putting a swift end to our choral endeavor.

In Podrouzo we discover an art gallery that is also a restaurant. The menu is tantalizing enough that my taste buds are having orgasms over the gazpacho soup, tortillas and zingy salad with cilantro and ginger. Delicioso! After dinner, we make a grocery store run for tomorrow's lunch. More gastronomic surprises.

I never thought that seeing just a couple of heads of broccoli and cauliflower would have me in ecstasy. I hold them and cuddle them. Shall I just buy and guzzle them raw? Too bad I have just eaten dinner. I break a tiny sliver off the broccoli. Ach, very bitter.

We find smoked salmon again. Lucky us! I pick up cheese, cukes and avos, and anchovy-filled green olives for tomorrow's lunch. I keep going back to commune with the cauliflower and broccoli.

"Here's looking at you, kid!" I finally say to the veggies.

Right outside the grocery store, Lucia is standing with a sack full of bananas. "For tomorrow," she says with a smile. She made it. *Thank you Mum for taking care of her.*

"How about your feet?" I ask.

The Spanish *farmacia* (pharmacy) is a wonderful institution. Anyone can go there with ailments like sore throats, rashes, cuts and bruises, and the staff will cheerfully fix you up, as they did our Italian friend. They put on new dressings and replenished her pain pills. She is ready for tomorrow. Her newly taped up feet do not fill me with confidence, nor does the unwieldy pack on her back, or the bag of bananas in her hand.

"*Buen Camino*," I say, my shorthand for *May the angels walk with you and carry you on their shoulders.*

Day 14: O Podrouzo to Lavacolla

Lavacolla is our last overnight before Santiago -- only six miles away. We are really stretching this out, but if we hadn't, I would have missed ogling the heads of broccoli and cauliflower.

The trail weaves in and out of forests of ancient oaks and immigrant eucalyptus, though the main road is never far away. The amount of graffiti increases exponentially. On mile marker after mile marker, someone has sprayed the words LOVE WINS, in the most unloving and ugly way. On some of them, the blood-colored paint dribbles down like red tears. In one tunnel, some taggers have left their loud, hideous squiggles, while others choose to tell the world what this journey has meant to them -- *I feel I've lived a whole life in one month. Camino has taught me to love more, live better, laugh louder and don't forget to forgive yourself. Thank you Camino.* Another person wrote -- *the most powerful thing I've learned on The Way is nearly everyone is good and we are all walking our different journeys on the same path. That, and look after your feet.*

On one unaccompanied cardboard scrap I read, *I'm walking without money. Please help me - go to my blog and give.*

I walk by as judgmentally as I would a beggar in the city streets of my home town. And the same guilt bedevils me. To give or not to give? At home, I alleviate my guilt by donating to the food bank or the local homeless shelter. *There, see, I did something for those who are really in need, but damned if I will give you money directly.*

On the Camino I wonder if it is meant to be part of someone's pilgrim's journey to live off alms. The "Go to my website and give" does not inspire kindness to do so, but I do hope they didn't go to bed hungry that night, or that my lunch doesn't turn into stone. My own journey so far has not made me generous.

In the same tunnel, I see another scrap of cardboard, same message, different pilgrim, and then another with a small can in front of it. Where are these people? Sitting at some fancy bar in Madrid, hitting refresh every few minutes to watch the money roll in? Well, not from this tight-wad. I dub this the Beggar's Tunnel.

As the landscape turns more urban, we find ourselves walking through the busy-ness of everyone else's lives. I long to be beamed directly to Santiago and to skip spending yet another night in another bed. We turn the corner into Los Alcazares, where the 12 Bar and Lounge, named so because it is exactly 12 kilometers to Santiago, is bursting at the seams with hikers and bikers. Aside from the bar, which no self-respecting hamlet is without, there is an inn and a locked church. I had this delusion that on the Camino, being a Catholic thing, there would be loads of churches along the way where we could take time out to contemplate. Apart from the big town cathedrals, which charge an entry fee if it isn't Sunday, the churches are pretty much locked up. Can't even take a peek.

Well, if I can't go to church, then my only choice is to stop at the bar. Like vultures, we hover to nab an outside table just as soon as it becomes vacant. I go in to order a large slice of the Torta de Santiago, and tea.

"Busy day," I say to the owner.

"This is nothing. Last week there were 2000 people a day coming through."

"2000 pilgrims, like with three zeros after the two and per day, not per week?"

"It is crazy in August. In September it changes - many more couples and single women. You are lucky. It's not so bad now."

As I sip my tea, I look up stats from the official Pilgrim Office website on my phone. It is my turn to say to David, "Did you know . . . that last year 327,342 pilgrims were received at the Pilgrimage Office, almost evenly split between men and women? 28% who received the *Compostela* were under 30, 55% were between 30 and 60 years old and 17% were over 60. That's us."

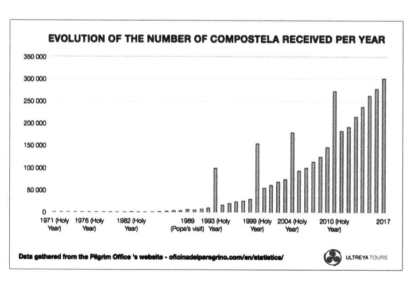

EVOLUTION OF THE NUMBER OF COMPOSTELA RECEIVED PER YEAR

Data gathered from the Pilgrim Office 's website - oficinadelperegrino.com/en/statistics/   ULTREYA TOURS

I dazzle him with other facts, like -- 44% of all pilgrims claim they completed the pilgrimage for solely religious reasons, and 60% walked the Francés.

"Oh wow! They have wonderful graphs and pie charts," I say, showing them to him.

"What's a Holy Year?" I ask my resident font of Catholic knowledge.

"A Holy Year is when the feast of St. James falls on a Sunday. They declare a plenary indulgence."

"Plenary Indulgence!" I say, "That sounds deliciously sinful."

"Actually for the Catholics who believe in that kind of thing, it's quite serious. All sins are forgiven, you won't go to either hell or purgatory. But you have to go to confession, take communion, and be sincerely sorry for your sinful ways. That is why you see enormous spikes for pilgrims during a Holy Year. It wipes clean your slate of sins."

I look back at the graphs on my phone. "Did you know that last year there were 50,000 more pilgrims than in the 2010 Holy Year? At one site it says that if the popularity of the Camino continues, they are expecting over half a million pilgrims for the 2021 Holy Year." I do some math in my head. This poor little bar will have 4000 visitors a day. Unfathomable!

I wonder why hardly anybody walked the Camino prior to the Nineties. "I thought loads of people have been making this journey for the last thousand years. That's not so?"

"Lots of people think that, but it's not true," says David. "The glorious heyday of the Santiago pilgrimage only lasted for about 300 years, from about the 11th to the 13th centuries. Then came the Little Ice Age, the Black Death, the Protestant Reformation, endless wars, and other things that dampened people's enthusiasm for long walks. And the trickle dried up almost completely when the bones disappeared."

"The bones disappeared? No kidding, somebody stole James' bones? Aren't they sealed in a crypt or something?"

"They were lost for almost 300 years. And you know whose fault it was?"

"The Democrats?"

"Sir Francis Drake."

"Francis Drake, the explorer?"

"Francis Drake, the pirate. He's not a cute and cuddly made-for-TV hero in this country. No, the bones were lost in 1589 when an English force under Drake sacked and burned the seaport town of A Coruña, just a long day's march north of Santiago. This was just a year or so after the disaster of the Spanish Armada, and the bishop at Santiago was so terrified of devil Drake that he hastily hid the holy relics and didn't tell anybody where they were. Word got out that the bones were lost, and the pilgrims pretty much stopped coming. They stayed away for almost 300 years.

"It wasn't until the late nineteenth century that people started walking again, after the remains were rediscovered and authenticated. But the numbers were small. It took another hundred years or so before the revival of the Camino as we know it. In many places the route was forgotten or the trail was impassable. One big step forward was when a dedicated priest and a bunch of volunteers with yellow paint began marking arrows on trees, buildings, fence posts, rocks, anything to point the way. In fact, there's a great story about when the priest was painting yellow arrows in the Pyrenees near the border. He was stopped by the Civil Guards, who naturally asked what the hell he was doing. His answer? "I am preparing a great invasion from France.""

"That was in the mid-'80s, and things picked up speed after that. The Camino was dubbed the first European Cultural Route in 1987, the Pope visited in 1989, and it became a UN World Heritage site in 1993. The EU chips in with grants to help maintain the trails. I reckon historians are going to look back on this time, right now, as the second great flowering of the Camino."

* * * * *

We are less than half an hour away from our next hotel. Fortified by the caffeine and sugar infusion, it is on with our packs and off we go. Suburban streets with gracious new homes and pedicured gardens give way to row housing with postage stamp size yards, which in turn fade into plain old concrete apartment buildings. Intermingled are many remnants of ancient homes at all levels of dilapidation and renovation, roofs falling in and moss eroding the structures.

The temperature is already in the nineties. By now many of the mileage markers are missing -- the metal plates that show the distance to Santiago have long since been harvested for souvenirs. *Are we there yet?* My body downshifts into a super slow mode. If I go any slower, I will drown in my own puddle of sweat. Faster, more agile walkers leaving a trail of *Buen Caminos* shame me into speeding up a little. *The faster you walk, the quicker you'll get there*, I tell myself, and swing my walking sticks more vigorously, as though I am cross-country skiing. Finally we arrive at Lavacolla. It's 11 AM on a Sunday, and the church bells are pealing.

Lavacolla

We aren't about to clear the pews by putting our sweaty, smelly bodies in there -- but just briefly, we hover about the church door and peek in. I feel like a gate-crashing imposter as the faithful in their Sunday best stream in, laughing, exchanging greetings and pecks on the cheek, totally ignoring us. As the service begins, we find some shade to sit under and chat with other perigrinos before our last push. The last mile is all uphill to our hotel, a restored and refashioned rural farmhouse.

How good the shower feels, and now with a cold beer in hand, we put our feet up on the terrace. I pull out my journal. It's been a couple of days since I've written anything. My brain is empty.

"Where were we yesterday?"

It is like I emptied the garbage can and something important got thrown out and is now irretrievable. I go through my pictures and review the stamps we have collected to jog my memory. Like doing a jigsaw puzzle, I piece it together to recreate the picture of the day before. I end my writing with *I am already sad that our Camino is drawing to a close. Despite the foot pain I have had to constantly nurse, I'm just getting into the swing of walking and look forward to each morning so much -- now we have only one more day. Maybe we should do the Portuguese Camino or walk around Mont Blanc next year.*

Tomorrow we will make our big entrance into Santiago de Compostela, where we hope to spend a few days. We still have another ten days to go before catching our onward flight. The plan is to rent a car and explore Northern Portugal. My mind races ahead to the future, wondering what, where and how.

At dinner I ask David, "So has the Camino met your expectations?"

"I'd like to do it again with a full pack and at full speed. Maybe I'll do that when you are traveling somewhere else."

My heart sinks. Gosh, he sacrificed his dream Camino for me, to walk with me at my pace and not as far. Sure he got to smell the cow pastures and he loved that, but still. Who knows if there will be a next time?

We have yet to come up with an itinerary for our last ten days. The Camino has truly kept us in the here and now; even tomorrow is too far away. That proverbial light bulb flashes in my head.

"Let's forget the driving holiday and keep walking," I say. "Would you like to walk to Finisterre, alone, without me?" Finisterre is another four days of walking at David's warp-speed.

"How about you?" he asks.

"Pleasure princess Asifa will hie herself to the beach, book some massages, get in some serious spa time, read, write and sip Sangria. She'll meet you in Finisterre."

David's eyes light up like a kid on Christmas day who'd received a surprise gift that he had longed for but was too shy to even ask.

www.ideasperegrinas.es

Together we pore over the map and come up with a plan.

While he is doing the extra 100 kilometers (62 miles) to Finisterre, I will bus it to Muxía, have two beach days, then walk the 20 miles between Muxía and Finisterre. There, hand in hand, we will walk the last few miles to the actual land's end.

I am excited. I am nervous. What will it be like to walk alone? Each of us plots and plans our routes, making reservations. I have this feeling that our real pilgrim walk is about to begin, each walking alone, pushing our own limits. My brain sends out a tickler, *Don't forget to restock your Ibuprofen supply.*

Day 15: Lavacolla to Santiago

We are on the road at the crack of dawn for that last eleven kilometer push to Santiago, through noise, highways, urban crowds, and squawking pedestrian crossing signals.

We climb Gozo Hill, the last viewpoint before the Cathedral. At the top there is the Monument of the Pilgrims -- a monument to us, to all those who have gone before us, and to all those who will come after. It's cluttered with shoes, shells, sticks and stones as well as messages and photos. From here we see the holy grail, the spires of the great Cathedral just four kilometers away.

It is the last green space to hang out and rest our weary limbs. We find a quiet spot and I pull out my apple, contemplating the faraway spires.

"I wonder just what Saint James would have preached, and in what language?"

"Weeeell actually, ..." David begins.

"Most likely James only spoke Aramaic. And given what we know about most Galileans during that period, James was

probably not literate. After all, he was a fisherman by trade. So, as a practical matter, how would he communicate with the Hispanics? Nobody knows, though at the Pentecost, when the Holy Spirit descended on the Apostles and they started to speak in tongues, legend has it that James was given the gift of Latin."

"The New Testament wasn't even written in 40 AD, right? So what did he preach?" I ask.

"You are right, Christianity as we know it didn't exist then. At best, there were only a few thousand Christians in the entire world. The first Gospel, Mark, was probably written in the late 60's AD, and the other gospels 20 to 30 years after that. Even the earliest of Paul's epistles – the earliest Christian scriptures we have – were written maybe half a dozen years after James was dead. So if Santiago carried any scripture at all with him in 40 AD, it would most likely be Jewish scripture, or writings about Jesus that have not come down to us. Maybe he just told personal stories about his remarkable friend and teacher."

"So James didn't speak the language, was probably illiterate, and had no gospel to preach. He was beheaded by Herod Agrippa in Jerusalem, and then his bones showed up back in Spain in a stone boat guided by angels. And millions, including us, have walked this Camino to ask for miracles in his name, and bypass hell and purgatory and go straight to heaven," I summarize, trying to absorb it all.

"All the stories are true, and some of them actually happened," says David. "That's not why we walk."

I'm in a trance as I stare at the magnificence of the Cathedral spires. I think of Dorothy, the Scarecrow and the Tin Man catching their first glimpse of the Emerald City. I'm filled with awe at our human need to believe in myths and miracles. See what it has created! I imagine the thurible swinging inside the church, billowing out the sweet smell of frankincense and myrrh. I imagine the Holy Spirit descending and carrying me to new heights of spiritual experience, taking me home. How badly I want that experience.

"Okay, let's do it," David commands, bringing me back to reality.

Modernity strips away any pilgrim euphoria I feel. Shall we check into the hotel and drop our packs off, or shall we head directly to the Cathedral? The multi-lane road disappears into a warren of alleyways. The Camino signs beckon our dragging feet to complete the journey that began 13 days ago, a lifetime.

Cafes, bars, panadarías, pastelerías, and a million billion pilgrim knick-knack shops splash gaudy made-in-China plastic souvenirs onto the cobbled streets. We are jostled by armies of tourists, distracted by the window shopping, the smell of coffee, and free samples of Torta de Santiago.

Crazy me, commerce is the last thing I expect. Somehow I have held an image of a whole pack of pilgrims, hundreds and hundreds of us, funneling through the narrow stone streets, like a procession, heading for the Cathedral. What happened to the 2000 pilgrims a day? Have they already been and gone as we dawdled in Podrouzo and Lavacolla? Are we really it? I don't see any other walkers, just masses of well dressed, clean tourists. Picking our way through the throng, I remember that there are other ways of coming to Santiago de Compostela, like by bus, air, and car.

We have walked 130 miles, make way for us, I want to say. *This is our journey, not yours.* We arrive at a tunnel where a bagpiper is piping. Two young women with backpacks and walking sticks come running past us. David says that is the custom, to run this last bit to the square. I didn't know that. Before I can even say, "let's do it," we are there. The girls are throwing their sticks up in the air, hugging each other and doing a victory jig. Click go the cameras, click, click, click.

We are frozen in place, awed by the Cathedral's façade. The square is mostly empty. A few other Camino walkers lie on the ground, using their packs and each other as pillows. It is the end for them. For us, feeling somewhat deflated, we search for the church's entrance to pay our respects to St. James. I so badly want to walk into a church where the priest swings his censer, and choirs of young boys in white robes sing Gregorian chants. I want a rite of passage, to be purified and sanctified.

A notice on the wall reads, "No backpacks, no sticks, go to the hostels and take a shower first." No, it doesn't say the latter. The line to get in is forever. Only 25 people at a time are let in, and you only get to stay for 25 minutes. What an inauspicious ending to our walk. Maybe the all-knowing God knows that I'm not really a pilgrim. No pomp and circumstance for me, just the busking bagpiper. But still, I have walked 130 miles on a bum foot. "Look Mum, I did it." "Yes," she whispers quietly. I smile and decide to celebrate the moment like the girls, holding my sticks up in the air, while David takes a picture. I do the same for him. We hug.

Tired and hungry, we look for our hotel. The room won't be ready until after 2 pm, but we can leave our bags. The receptionist tells us that the Blessing of the Pilgrims mass in the church is at noon and 7:30 pm every day. There is a different entrance.

The fact that the world really doesn't care about my accomplishments, or whether I exist or not, is humbling. After all, I am just one more perigrino, out of millions who have been here before and the millions who will follow. This is a well-trodden path, and I have to create my own glory if I want to bask in it.

We go to the Pilgrimage Center with our pilgrim *credencials* in hand for the final stamp and to pick up the certificate. We stand in line with dozens, backpacks still on their backs, their hair matted with sweat and dirt, waiting for our turn. This official end surprises me. It is the same electronic system I would expect to find at a major airport immigration hall. Every time an officer is available, the number of the booth flashes, directing the next in line to go there. When my number comes up, I find myself facing an older gentleman with a most empathetic smile.

"Where did you start your walk?" he asks.

"Ribadeo." I answer.

"Did you walk the whole way?"

"I did." . . . well, all but 10 kilometers, but I don't tell him that.

He flips through my *credencial*, studying my stamps.

"What was your reason for doing the Camino?"

Now this question poses an ethical problem. If I say Spiritual, I get the real *compostela,* but if I tell him I was just looking for a pleasurable adventure, I will only get a certificate of completion. In a flash, I think of the stone boat and the chances that it is just some random Roman who is actually buried in the Cathedral. That gives me the confidence to respond.

"It was a cultural and spiritual journey."

In gorgeous calligraphy, he writes my name on the *Compostela* and hands it to me, saying, "May the blessing of this journey live on in your heart and in your life." To that I say Amen.

Outside in the courtyard, hundreds have donated their walking sticks -- wooden ones, fancy metal ones, some their hats and shoes, including one pair of hiking sandals that is more duct tape than sandal. The sign says that this collection will one day become a sculpture, an ode to the pilgrims.

In French, German, English, Spanish and Polish, another sign points to the debriefing rooms. The hosts call themselves pilgrim companions. It is a place for sharing stories, consolidating memories. We go to the English room. It is just us and three companions.

"You experienced God Space," Noel, one of the companions, says when I tell the story of the footfalls and the magical butterfly experience. Those are definitely not the words I would have chosen. But these folks are true believers.

Noel, who has done umpteen caminos, goes on to tell us the story of a man he met and walked with a very long time ago. "That man," he says, "gave me strength and courage to keep walking when I was on the verge of giving up." They stayed in touch for several years and then their lives drifted apart. Seven years later, Noel, on the spur of the moment, decided to walk a more remote camino.

"At one point, I went off the trail and clambered down to sit on a rock. Now this was truly off the beaten path. Someone else was already there." He paused for a moment. "The next thing I knew, the stranger turned around to look at me and said, 'Hello, Noel!'

"It was the same man I had lost touch with. What are the odds? That is God Space," he said.

Noel walks and walks, because it is in these long distance walks that he experiences moments that take his breath away. Indeed, for me too. I find myself chasing experiences, pushing my limits physically, emotionally and spiritually, because it opens me up to moments when I connect to our amazing Universe so deeply, that I feel ethereal -- me a tiny speck of stardust that emanated from the Big Bang.

This ends the official part of our walk, except for attending the pilgrim's mass at 7:30 pm at the Cathedral, when I will finally get my spectacle of the priests swinging the censers.

Until then, we have an anniversary to celebrate -- number 43. It's a scary number of years to be married. That's how long parents and grandparents are married for, not me! But here we are in our sixties. We have just done a long walk. It's time to treat ourselves to something very special.

Sitting at the very end of the pilgrimage trail, next to the Cathedral, is the Hostal dos Reis Católicos, a fifteenth century hospital now turned into one of the most luxurious hotels in Spain. Driven by piety, economic and political might, Ferdinand and Isabel issued a royal command to build this hostel-hospital. I didn't know it, but they too did a pilgrimage to Santiago. I am delighted to be in such good company. We dine on multiple courses in the medieval stone chamber, which back then was the hospital morgue. Today it is a restaurant extraordinaire.

"Did you know," said David, "The words *hotel, hostel* and *hospital* share the same Latin root, *hospes,* meaning guest?"

It's that Catholic school education bubbling up again, I think but don't say.

"Nowadays those words have different meanings, but at the time when this was built, the idea of a hostel included a bed, food, as well as care for wounded feet and anything else that ailed you."

We lick the last forkful of the cheese cake with hazelnut ice cream, down the Grappa, and now our lids droop, begging for a nap.

At 7 pm the church bells sound, and we are there, ready to be among the first to enter as the imposing doors swing open to let us in. The golden altar blows me away. It is blinding. It is awe-strikingly beautiful. St. James looks like Midas. The huge censer hangs from a pulley in the ceiling of the cupola. There is enough gold and silver there to support the entire world's refugee population, and they would still get some change back.

"Let us pray," the priest must be saying, for the whole congregation stands up, and with bowed heads, they mumble something in Spanish that probably means, "Lord hear our prayer."

I love rituals, especially sacred ones. This Mass, despite my secular beliefs, allows me to continue to bask in my I-have-completed-the-pilgrimage glory. I am open for an out-of-body experience. It is a lovely service in a magnificent setting, organ music resounding within the towering walls. I don't quite follow the sermon, but I think the priest is saying something like, "Your pilgrimage does not stop here. The bigger journey of following Christ's footsteps has only just begun. *Buen Camino* for the rest of your lives. He walks with you. Make your journey a worthy one."

Oddly enough, as I sit quietly in the pew, I find myself praying to St. James. "Please bless all of us pilgrims of life, searching for answers. Please give us the strength and the courage to be bigger than ourselves, to be more compassionate, more patient. Allow us to fill the world with our laughter. Allow us to receive wisdom from wherever it comes. . . and thank you for enabling me to complete this walk, despite my bum foot. I am grateful to the butterflies that led the way, the footfalls that accompanied me. Thank you, Santiago. Thank you Universe. I am so lucky to be alive."

The service ends. The thurible, or as the Spanish call it, *bota-fumiero* -- literally means smoke expeller -- is still fastened. There is no sign that the priests are going to bathe us in incense. I ask the German girl next to me "When will they swing the censer?"

"Only when you pay for it!" comes the answer.

"What!" I feel so cheated.

"God does a retail business in the Catholic Church," David jumps in, equally disappointed.

We come out of the church and there in the square is Lucia, without her backpack and bananas, absolutely beaming.

"Were you at Mass?"

She had gone to the noontime one, and guess what? The priests swung the giant censer. Lucky her! Hers was a true pilgrimage. She fulfilled the promise she had made to God. She deserved the full pomp and circumstance. I am so happy, happy for her. Seems this God knows the wheat from the chaff.

I Walk Alone

"Text me as soon as you get to your first stop, just so that I know you arrived safely," I say to David as we part company in the morning.

"Are you sure you don't want me to download the maps and apps on your phone?" David asks me yet again.

"No, I mean yes, I'm sure." I really want to be guided by serendipity and my intuition, which would probably sound quite foolish to him.

We bid each other *Buen Camino* as he hits the trail to Finisterre and I hoof it to the bus station, headed for Muxía. My backpack will be delivered to the hotel by Correos.

Muxía

Traveling yanks me out of my routine. In the middle of the night, I wake up wanting to pee. I bang into furniture, and in my half sleep try to remember where in this particular bathroom the toilet is. I sit on the edge of what I think is the toilet. It turns out to be the tub. Too late. That's the negative side of sleeping in a different place every night.

And yet, this same unfamiliarity awakens my senses. The golden sunrises are more golden, the seagulls riding the thermals elate me. Even the smell of frying *churros* -- a kind of donut -- gives me the happy tingles.

This morning I am enjoying the sun being born, popping up from behind the horizon, lighting up the hills that rise up from the Atlantic. The town of Muxía still sleeps, except for the fish mongers, the fruit sellers, and the clothing merchants who are setting up for market day. I am the lone browser, who is taken aback at what I see in a large vat full of water.

Dead octopuses. They lie deflated, one on top of another, like blobs of dark-grey jello with eyes and spiny hair sticking out. There must be fifty or sixty of them. I ate part of one last night for dinner. It was absolutely delicious, but seeing a gelatinous mass of them makes my stomach churn in a way that kills the appetite for an encore meal.

It's a soft, gentle day. Not a cloud in the sky. I meditate to the rhythmic music of waves breaking on the rocky coast at low tide. I have the whole day ahead of me with absolutely nothing planned. I scramble along the cobblestone walkway, through the old town, towards a spot at the tip of the peninsula. There, right above the rocks where the surf breaks, is the Church of the Señora de la Barca, our Lady of the Boat. This is yet another zero kilometer marker of the Camino. A tourist magnet.

Who is this Lady of the Boat? I don't have my very own Wikipedia, David, to ask, so to Google I go and surf endless entries.

Legend has it that the mother of Jesus arrived here in a stone boat, where she met St. James to console and encourage him in his preaching throughout Spain. The granite stones that surround the sanctuary are said to be the sail, the helm and the very boat itself that the Virgin came in. As though these kazillion ton boulders were a 3-D jigsaw puzzle, I try with all my imagination to think out of the box and reconstruct the stone boat. Just can't see it. Did her boat capsize and break apart? How did she get back? And what's with all these stone boats anyway?

Google leaves me with even more questions than answers. But then divine miracles are just that, aren't they? The proof lies in the hearts of the faithful, and not on the internet.

I do discover that this same spot was sacred to the Celts who lived along this coast. Christianity has always had a way of co-opting sacred sites and legends belonging to the local "heathens," and incorporating them into its own mythology. It doesn't surprise me that a hermitage was built here in the twelfth century. The church, which was constructed and dedicated to the Virgin in the seventeenth century, on Christmas Day of 2013 was struck by lightning and mostly destroyed by the fire that ensued. What would make God angry enough to destroy a fine church on his son's birthday?

Divine providence or not, they have done a wonderful job restoring this popular place of worship. Sailors, fishermen, and all those for whom the ocean is important, come here to ask for blessings from the Señora de la Barca.

I look for the famous Pedra dos Abalar or Rocking Stone, the one that heals diseases, induces fertility, or determines guilt versus innocence. I try to match the google photo of it with what I actually see, but I can't identify it among the enormous rocks that are strewn out to sea. The drama the waves create as they alternately crash and cradle the rocks is mesmerizing. This, and the doleful sound of the wind singing, invokes a feeling of intimacy with the land, the rocks, the sanctuary and the sea. It is not difficult to believe that this place has been steeped in legends since the beginning of time.

While my spiritual glass is frothing over, my stomach growls with hunger. Walking along the waterfront back into town, I see ads hawking, "Pilgrim Breakfast 8 Euros". This includes eggs, toast and coffee. The memory of our very first day on the trail, when David wanted to indulge and my fears kept us from doing so, flits across my radar. How far I've come since that day. Here I am, two weeks later, walking alone with confidence. I go in and order the 10 Euro breakfast, which includes a ham and cheese omelet. Have to have the required daily intake of ham, while in Spain.

Intense pain wakes me up from my afternoon nap. I have forgotten to take Ibuprofen, and the inflammation is back with a vengeance. When the pain subsides, I kick off my shoes and walk barefoot along the frothy edge of the chilly Atlantic, letting the lapping water bathe and massage my aching feet. The cold numbs all that ails me. I perch on a rock, listen to the songs of the sea, and picnic on the pre-prepared supermarket salad, guacamole and bread that I had picked up. A glass of cham-pagne would have been perfect, but it's so hard to get rock-side service here.

The mighty sun is about to dissolve into the ocean, and it lures me to dash over to the western side of the peninsula, which I do.

I don't know what it is about this sunset that makes me feel that the show is being put on just for me. My eyes tear up with joy as a deep-seated gratitude for being alive wells up. I don't need priests swinging censers to purify and sanctify me with aromatic smoke. . . the Universe is doing that all in her own way.

I am ready to walk the next 20 miles over the mountain to meet up with David in Finisterre -- the end of the earth, so called by the Romans. According to legend, long before the Romans, Finisterre was a sacred location for the Celts who came to worship at the altar of the sun -- Ara Solis. Today it is still a popular finishing point of the extended Camino, a place where pilgrims take selfies at the zero mile marker, watch the sunset, burn their clothes, and jump into the chilly ocean for the ultimate cleansing or baptism into their new lives.

With heady contentment, I stroll back to the hotel to get an early night before my long walk alone tomorrow.

"HA!" says the devil. It's fiesta week in Muxía, and partiers are just beginning to arrive. It is 9:30 pm. The light is waning. The luminary decorations that span the streets turn on, and the drum beat of amplified rock music begins. Nobody is sleeping tonight. I set my alarm for 7 am, just in case I do nod off.

Who am I kidding? Waves of drunkards screech, shout, laugh, sing and quarrel at full lung power just under my window. Of course they wait for me to drift off, to come by and punch my sleep away.

Finally, the day breaks and I can move on. A group of kids comes in for breakfast, emanating bleary drunkenness. A young woman falls into my lap, sending my cup of hot tea flying. She staggers towards another chair, totally misses, and flops on the floor next to me. She starts to paw me, mouthing something in

Galician, or is her Spanish so slurred that I cannot make head or tail of a single word?

With my best stern school teacher voice I say, "No hablo Español."

"Engleeesh?" she asks. I have to nod.

"I love you, I love you," she says and then asks the proprietor for a drink.

"Pay first," he says, but I can see he is really reluctant to give this child-woman another drink. The group of boys she is with laughs nervously, and not one of them gets up to rescue her. I down what is left of my tea and walk off into the sunrise, leaving the drunkards for the barman to deal with.

Muxía to Lires

The chilly air bites my face. Watching my pace, no one would ever guess that I hardly slept. But it's a beautiful morning, and I'm doing what I have come to love doing best, walking.

Today I don't hear any footfalls. *Mum, where are you? Are you coming with me?* Fear and excitement lurk within me, like a kid who is leaving home for the first time.

"You are no longer a Camino virgin, you can do it. You don't need me anymore," a voice whispers.

But, but, what if I get lost? What if I see a snake, or twist my ankle? What if I lack the stamina to climb this mountain alone? What if . . .?

An older couple catches up with me, and they slow down to walk alongside. *Thank you mum.* Obviously she sent them to let me know I wasn't alone. In life, she truly believed that God sent angels when you need them most. Every time she fell, someone -- *an angel* -- would be there to help. People would pop out of nowhere to help carry her groceries, or in the days when she drove, she was convinced that God always found her a good parking place. It was true, she had the best parking karma ever. To her, God was the grand conductor orchestrating what I would call coincidences and what she saw as miracles. I dismissed her miracles back then, and now here I am thanking her for sending this couple along. I can only laugh at the irony.

The couple are from the Grand Canaries. "Walking is our meditation retreat," they tell me, in their cobbled together Spanglish. "We take walking holidays every year." We deplete our vocabularies in each other's language very quickly, and after bidding me a *Buen Camino* they speed ahead.

As I leave the main road and turn into the forest, eucalyptus aromas spiked with the sweet and sour smell of over-ripe guavas twist my nose. It takes me back to Hawaii, where I lived for ten years. Rotting guavas, how I hated that smell then! The memory of uprooting the hundreds of seedlings that each of the fallen fruit would spawn, taking over the garden, makes me shudder. But here I search for a ripe one, to suck on its sweet nectar. I forget that I'm in for a long day of walking, and chase skittery butterflies while climbing 900 feet. I am not huffing or puffing at all. My legs must be getting stronger, though I must express my disappointment. After 130 miles of walking, my cauliflower thighs are showing no signs of smoothing out or firming up.

What was it that David was telling me, about some twelfth century pope spouting something about walking and weight loss? I shall have to text him tonight.

In no time I am at the top, eye to eye with the windmills, the whole world stretching out to the horizon. I wonder why these metal giants stand still, despite the wind. There is not another walker in sight. As I step off the trail to a wide open space, I am dancing with the wind, prancing like a deer, singing like Julie Andrews -- well, I am, in my head.

Climb every mountain, ford every stream, follow every rainbow until you find your dream.

I tarry a little longer to inhale the moment, this view and this wonderful feeling that Galicia belongs all to me. The hardest part of the walk is already behind me. There are a few more smaller hills ahead, but it doesn't matter, as I have grown wings! I simply fly down until a sight, way down the road, stops me dead in my tracks. It is an oversized colored umbrella perched on a white box. But I am in the middle of nowhere. There's not a single farmhouse in sight for miles around. I come closer, and sure enough there is a woman who has set up a small table. She has a large thermos of coffee, a basket of fruit, a plateful of homemade cake, and an outsized jar with a tap, filled with icy home-concocted juice. She also has a stamp and ink pad to validate passing pilgrims' passports, as well as a couple of beach chairs where I can rest my weary body. A small basket welcomes any contribution I wish to make.

She tells me a friend drives her up here where she sets up the service stall. "I can't walk, but I can catch blessings by serving the pilgrims," she says. The iced mixture of juices and herbs is nectar to my throat on this sweltering day.

Just five more miles to go. By now the Muxía-bound walkers who began in Lires or even Finisterre are coming at me. "*Buen Camino,*" we nod to each other without breaking our pace. One couple I meet at a cafe had left Finisterre early this morning. They described it as a party town, a place to celebrate the end of their Camino. "Muxía, on the other hand, is a quiet gentle place to watch the sunset and sunrise. A good place to wind down before returning home," they say. I wonder if they know about the eardrum-bursting music, drunkenness, and the unruliness of the town during fiesta time? Should I let on?

It is not for me to say, it is for them to find out. That's what this walk of hundreds of miles is all about.

How I love pine forests for the cushion of soft needles they lay for me to walk on. My feet are ecstatic. I pass more folks and linger to chat. I'm in no hurry to reach Lires. I stop to hear stories from the Italian pilgrim, Alberto, whom I have just met.

"I recently turned 50. I have been working for the same company for 30 years, and the Camino just called to me," he says. "It was time to quit and start something new, so I did, and I'm so happy. It has been a road full of small miracles."

"Really! Like what?" I enquire.

"I was talking to a German woman and then continued on ahead of her. As I walked, I wondered *How do you say Buen Camino in German?* So I turned around and walked back 500 meters to ask the lady. You know, my sun glasses and one of my shoes had fallen off the back of my pack. If I hadn't turned back, I wouldn't have noticed. Amazing how the gods are taking care of me." He would have got along just fine with my mum.

"So how *do* you say Buen Camino in German?" I ask.

"There's no real translation." He then tells me about a very old lady he met. "She is carrying the bones of her mother to Santiago. She is walking very slowly, so it will take her many months before she comes to Santiago. Incredible. So many beautiful pilgrims. And now I meet you from Tanzania."

I say "Tanzania" when people ask me where I'm from. It is the place of my birth, the place where I took my first breath, the place that remains the home of my heart. Hardly anybody has met someone from Tanzania. What excitement that brings to the conversation. Very different from saying I'm from Los Estados Unidos, which always freezes the conversation, not necessarily in a hostile way at all, just mundane.

One of the joys of walking alone is I don't have to share conversations with my husband where he unwittingly hijacks it into a different direction, interjecting his did-you-know stories while I stand aside and listen. We are curious about very different things. The other joy of walking alone is the silence. My thoughts stay in my own head, and as I take in new sensory input, I feel myself dissolving into my walk. It is entirely my experience, not influenced by another's eyes, ears or nose. I'm feeling lucky, happy and complete.

Too quickly I come to Lires, where I am to stay a couple of nights. There's a trail map near the Church which shows a circular ten-kilometer Nature hike on a local coastal trail. I will do that tomorrow and then come back and go to the beach, I promise myself.

For now I hear the ocean calling. I amble along the river path. Just watching birds swoop and land with such finesse is witnessing grace. Here on the Lires River, where flocks of birds float, fish, and fly around, I am privy to the most amazing avian aerial dance performance. There is either a fish farm or some processing plant nearby, which acts as a powerful magnet for the seagulls who crowd every available perch. From there they squabble and squawk about who knows what. When I turn the corner, my eyes widen, and for a moment I forget to breathe.

The Atlantic Ocean is at my feet, emerald, azure and inky blue, lapping at the white sand beach. The sun is low in the sky and as red as red can be, hot from a day's work of bringing us light. It is time for it to take a dip in the ocean. I drink in the fiery drama of crimson beauty as the light and the color linger even as they fade. It is 9:15 at night, the close of another day.

I return to my casa, and sure enough there's a text from David.

"Do you mean Pope Calixtus ll, the one who put his name to the Codex Calixtinus?"

Hell if I know what I mean. But then another text comes in. "I think the quote you are looking for is: The Camino pilgrimage... takes us away from luscious foods, it makes gluttonous fatness vanish, ... it cleanses the spirit, leads us to contemplation, humbles the haughty, raises up the lowly, loves poverty."

The man, I mean my husband, is a genius. The only bit of the quote that had stuck with me was "it makes gluttonous fatness vanish." It didn't for me. Maybe I've eaten too many *boccadillos*.

Lires - the Nature Walk

I love the way my host family hangs out with me as I breakfast on tea, toast and homemade cake. On the Camino so far, I've seen no chain hotels, no KFCs or Burger Kings to meet the pilgrims' needs. There are no employees dressed in corporate-sanctioned clothing, having scripted conversations: "Thank you for choosing us. Have a nice day." There is no brand in these casas rurales, albergues and inns. Mama is out there with her workaday apron. She tells me her husband is in hospital. He fell. She points to her rib cage and holds up nine fingers. I surmise he has broken nine ribs and his shoulder too. She looks at my passport and squeals in delight, "Mismo cumpleaños." We share the same birthday.

I tell her that I'm going to walk the coastal nature trail today. "No, no, está peligroso!" She calls her daughter, who speaks better English, to warn me that the route in places is very narrow and teeter-totters on the edge of a cliff. "Better you take the regular Camino. Much safer."

She detects my determination. "Take my phone number. Call me if something happens," She says. "You have water?" She gives me an extra piece of cake. I give her a big hug. For that moment we are sisters who deeply care for each other.

No corporate peon can act like that. They'd serve me breakfast and send me off with a "Have a nice day." I had not realized that by walking the Camino, I would be taking a major break from the corporate world -- or rather, I had not realized how much of my reality was defined by faceless corporations that pay people to be polite and nice to you. I realize just how much humanity has been sucked out of my daily life at home.

It is still early. Just 8:30 am. The sun has only just come up as I step out into the promise of the early morning that I have so come to love. Since I'm just doing a short walk and am returning to Lires, I put on my runners instead of my hiking boots, and in the wake of the long conversation, I forget to take my walking sticks.

Like a ballerina I walk, tip-toeing through the trails, not wanting to disturb the insects, the birds. Rabbits scuttle into their holes. Dragonflies dry their wings on the rocks. Flies buzz, landing on my nose and ears, wrenching the bliss out of me. "Go find a cow," I scold, swatting them off my body. In between fly swats, I drift back into my dream world and continue on the trail where the ocean pounds on the steep cliffs below and blackberry bushes offer me their fruit. It is the noisy quietness of Nature at work. The sea gulls are catching air currents, gliding up and down as though swinging on an invisible hammock.

The path gets narrower and is descending. Is this the part that my hostess warned me about? I stop to breathe in the ocean air, and then turn around to retrace my steps. Just then a group of twenty or so hikers, all with heavy back packs, big boots and walking poles in hand, come marching by. They look like the kind of people who could climb Everest before breakfast. They roar by me, leaving me drenched in their dust.

Well, if they are taking the trail, then so can I, I reason. Plumped up with courage and hope, I march in their footsteps over stone walls, down into the wooded valley and up the next ridge, where the beach is immediately below me. I watch the hikers artfully tumble down the hillside to the beach like a small avalanche of boulders. They kick off their shoes, throw off their packs, strip down to their underwear and jump into the icy waves. All that testosterone.

I decide to head back. But instead of retracing my footsteps, I take a trail which looks like it will lead me inland to the main Camino. From there it will be a straight shot back. The sun is scorching hot, and I'm ready for something to eat. I reckon I am just another hour away from an icy glass of Sangria.

The trail is getting narrower and narrower and turns steeply ocean-ward. Thorny bushes bite into my pants and into the flesh of my arms. Above and to my right I can see a tall pole with trail markings. I know I am on the right path, even though it is overgrown with blackberry vines and several other species of thorny bushes. *It's only a short distance and will end soon,* I tell myself. Just by sight, I trace where I think the path goes. It descends before it ascends towards the pole. I carefully and gingerly climb down towards a clear space that I can see, extricating myself from the clasp of thorns, one thorn at a time. I feel like I'm being swallowed by the Briar Patch; with each step, the brambles bite and slide me down their digestive tracts. *I can do it. I can do it. I can get myself out of here.* I have no clue how much time is passing. When I find a flat spot that will hold both my feet at once, I stand upright and survey the landscape.

Holy Shit, I'm on the edge of a precipice, a truly steep drop-off to where the ocean bashes the rocks. I'm not afraid of heights, but the fear of falling . . . I cannot breathe. I can see the pole with the trail markings above me. *I can do it. I can make it. Mummy, God, whoever, please help me, give me courage,* I pray.

I turn slowly to face the upward slope. A butterfly stops for a moment before flitting off. Hope -- that is hope, that's my dad saying he is looking out for me.

Then I notice a cluster of blackberries, bursting with ripeness. The picture of the Buddhist monk being chased by a lion, having to choose between being eaten or falling off a precipice, flits through my mind. The lion is closing in and the monk falls. A protruding branch catches his robe, breaking his fall. He sees a ripe strawberry, growing out of the hill. He plucks it and savors it as the branch that's holding him breaks off.

Might as well enjoy the blackberries.

I climb one insecure step after another, slipping a little, grabbing a thorny branch to steady myself. I'm thinking of the briar patch as my savior now. It will hold me and keep me from tumbling down onto the rocks below, even if it is shredding my flesh and my clothes.

Another butterfly. More hope.

A vulture flies above me, despair.

Breathe Asifa, breathe.

My calves hurt so badly. They are spasming and quivering so much that my heels clap up and down.

Stop. Breathe. You can do it.

A young kid appears out of nowhere, right above me. He looks at me for a moment, curious about what this old grey-haired lady is doing. He points to something below me. "Oh God, my phone. I've dropped my phone." It must have fallen out of my pocket.

He must have seen the despair in my eyes. In a jiffy he jumps down, retrieves my phone and gives it to me. With ease and agility he climbs a couple of steps up and then disappears. He is my omen. He is my hope. I know now that I'm just a couple of feet from a trail that I can't see, but is directly above me. If he can do it then so can I.

Yes, I did it. I am on higher ground now, with a clear trail ahead. That swig of water is the best champagne ever. Bottoms up, I empty my flask.

The ground is firm, flat, and free of brambles. I march back, hot sun or not, no smelling the flowers, no noticing anything. I'm walking so fast that even the flies are keeping out of my way. I'm hot. I'm tired. I'm hungry. That extra piece of cake that Mamma gave me -- I stuff it in my mouth. It's instant sustenance. I keep walking. I'm on the main trail that runs between Finisterre and Lires. The mile marker says five kilometers. I still have another hour to go, with no water.

I spy a bar perched high on the cliff, facing the beach and the horizon. It becomes my destination.

Finally I'm there. All I can do now is to collapse into a chair, sip cold beer, and suck on a plateful of langostinos that comes with a baguette and salad. Thank goodness for credit cards. This little indulgence cost $40, but I don't care. And I don't care that I'm the scruffiest patron there. Everyone else is in their Sunday best.

Reflections on the Briar Patch

I wash my clothes, my shoes and my body, checking for damage. My socks find a grave in the waste bin. My pants show signs of design alterations -- tiny little threads that have been pulled and broken from the tight weave of the synthetic fabric. They hang loosely, like untidy, unplanned tassels. I still have a month of traveling ahead of me. I cannot throw away the pants. Just have to wash the black dirt out. My skin is tattooed with tiny red bubbles of pinpricks and splodges of black and blue bruises. They do not speak of a harrowing experience. Really and truly, I am not the worse for wear.

Was all that pain and suffering in my head? Didn't I create my own vultures and hungry lion melodramas?

No, it was not at all comfortable walking through the path of thorns. In fact, it was downright painful, but that did pass. As Sylvia Boorstein said, "Pain is a part of life, but suffering is optional." Fear did cause me unnecessary suffering. It could have also lead to a more tragic outcome. But then, the boy showed up. Hope trumped fear and I've returned believing in angels. My mum was right again. Thank you so much, young boy. I shall try to pay your kindness forward.

Lires to Finisterre

No dilly-dallying to watch the mist slow-dance with the hills this morning. After yesterday's adventure, I just want to get to Finisterre and be done with this walk. I barely take in the beautiful countryside tamed by farms, cut up in geometrical shapes, until a Goddess moment arrests me. The sun, still low in the sky, bursts through a pine forest, its rays fanning out in a full circle. I have seen many a photograph of scenes just like this, captured by brilliant photographers. But to be standing, catching the rays that light the valley floor with rusts, oranges, reds, and hints of blue is exactly what I imagine sitting at the end of a rainbow would be like. I have a sense of being bathed in starlight emanating from our earth's very own star.

You've got 10 miles ahead of you. Get moving girl, my brain prompts. And so I do, gliding through the landscape. A couple of hours pass. I have no idea how far I have come or how far I have yet to go. There are absolutely no Camino markers. I study the map to gauge where I am and guesstimate the distance. It is a silly exercise, as the schematic representation of the route is not to scale. I have no bars on my phone to pull up Google Maps. I am getting weary and want to be there already. How I wish I had let David put the apps and maps on my phone.

Fortunately, it's not long before farmsteads turn into stone and concrete buildings, stuck together so tightly, there is little breathing room. Laundry hangs from windows, rather than clotheslines in the garden. The silence is now filled with car engines. It's almost noon, and the temperature is rising. A comfy seat in an air-conditioned bar would be so welcome. I keep walking. 5.6 kilometers shows up on the Camino mileage marker. That's the first one I have seen -- but I know this distance is to the end of the world - del fin del mundo, to the zero mile marker. Our hotel is way before that. I'm close.

Now that I'm in town, I pull up Google Maps. Fifteen minutes away, it says. Yay, I'm almost there! It shows a road going straight, which I assume is in the direction I'm going.

Bleep, bleep! A text from David.

Checking into the hotel, sitting on the beach, waiting for you.

I check Google maps again. 20 minutes away. Sh . . ugar, I'm going in the wrong direction. This time I turn the GPS on and let it take me to the hotel and David.

Cold beer, fresh-caught sardines grilled to perfection, a cool ocean breeze and a cheery waitress, reunion with David -- happy days are here again. A long nap to look forward to, a walk on the beach, feet in the cold Atlantic water, Nature's own spa.

In the last five days, while I found solitude, David found his Camino family of two Germans, a Hungarian and three Italians. They shared a dorm room together and played leap frog on the trail. He was so excited, walking at his own speed and doing the 60 miles his way. We show each other our pictures and tell our stories. Tomorrow, we will walk the last four kilometers together and watch the sunrise.

Finisterre is riddled with narrow winding streets, with buildings crawling and sprawling up the hillsides like barnacles on the side of a whale. Clothing stores display harem pants and elephant-covered Indian cotton skirts. Rastas, bearded, bedraggled and bare-footed, are just hanging out, their very worn backpacks and bed rolls slumped next to them. The town is full of young people living out their dreams, celebrating their freedom from conventional life. They are disconnected from the expectations of family, and have cut off cultural and corporate tethers. Walking the Camino has empowered them in a new way -- they are capable of living on very little. They have found a new family, the Camino family, a shared experience of walking hundreds upon hundreds of miles that binds them. Nobody else would truly understand.

When I was their age, I lived in a commune in London, taking on the cause of homelessness at a time when thousands of buildings lay vacant in London. In fact, David and I squatted in some of those buildings. I remember the delicious freedom of being un-tethered from my family and other conventional ties. It was a rite of passage. It's probably the same for these Camino walkers.

The Last Four Kilometers.

Hand in hand, David and I walk at dawn on deserted streets to the lighthouse that marks the end of the Earth. The tide is out, the waves are calm. The street lights are still on. The sun pops up without any colorful pomp and circumstance. I search for something extraordinary, I'm not sure what. I want some sign, an omen, something, anything. Is this it, nothing more than a pretty sunrise and the good feeling that we have completed what we had set out to do? We take pictures at the most photographed mile marker here: 0.000. What a humble and quiet ending to the walk.

We return for one last breakfast at the hotel. The buffet is the usual array of pastries, ham and cheese, and loaves of sliced, squishy sandwich bread on trays. Camino walkers are spread across the breakfast room and terrace. We casually joke about the ham and cheese. We don't know each other, but yet our hearts and minds are connected, having shared the same powerful experience. All our lives are in transition. We are drawn to each other, anxious to hold onto to this last shared Camino moment.

"What experience challenged you most on the trail?" I ask Sallye from Long Beach, who had walked the del Norte all the way from Irun in France.

"I discovered my inner fear of cows."

"Cows!" We laugh. Bovinophobia, who knew there was such a thing?

She twists her shoulder length, sun-bleached hair into a scrunchy, and then leans forward and relaxes into her elbows on the table. "I was totally exhausted and disgusted. All the beds were booked solid. I was totally ticked off that I had to walk another fifteen kilometers to find a place to sleep. I was so ready to quit and go surfing instead. And what did I run into on the trail?"

"A cow?" I offer.

"Yes, a cow, but not just any old cow. This one . . . she was shaking her head -- like don't you dare cross my path. I froze and glared at the stupid animal."

I watch Sallye's eyes stare out into the distance, in the way that you do when you relive a memory.

She tells us that she backed off a little and pulled out her guide book to see what it had to say about cows. "They should be no trouble, unless you come between a mother and her calf. Just keep walking," it advised. She slowly took a couple of steps forward. The cow just as quickly raised her head and stepped forward too, giving that vigorous shake of the head that says in no uncertain terms, "Last warning!"

"I stepped back several steps. Now what do I f-ing do? There was absolutely no one else around. Here I was, in the middle of the pasture, with a very disgruntled cow standing bang in the middle of the Camino path." She pauses.

No longer able to bear the suspense, we ask in unison, "Well, what did you do?"

"I googled cows," she says. "I actually had a signal."

I'm in awe that she even thought to do that.

"Did you know that more people are trampled to death by cows than are attacked by sharks?" Then very casually she says, "Last year there were 27 deaths by cow attack, versus four by sharks. That did not make me feel any better. I really didn't want to be trampled to death by a cow in the middle of nowhere in Spain."

Exhausted, terrified and angry, she retraced her steps. "Thank God for my Camino app. Luckily there was an alternate route into town I could take. All this for one stupid, disgruntled cow.

"When I finally got into town," she says with a smirk, "I ordered a big fat steak for dinner."

Wow! That's a hard story to top.

"What's next for you?" I ask her.

"I'm going to a surf yoga camp in Morocco, and then on to Peru to start a new life. I'll figure out a way to support myself."

That's my kind of lady.

The conversation moves on to a Brazilian from Sao Paulo. "I did three caminos back to back - the Francés, the Portuguese and the Primitivo," he says.

"How many days for the Francés?" the Bulgarian lady at the next table wants to know.

"Twenty-one, twenty-two, I don't remember."

The Bulgarian's eyes widen. She is so proud of her 26 day, 500 mile walk, but right at this moment she just whispers, "I did it in 26."

I'm completely impressed, because that involved crossing the Pyrenees, which is no mean feat. We took 14 days for less than 200 miles. I'm not sure I want to share that, but they ask the perennial questions: Which Camino? How far? And how long? I tell them, but add with much alacrity, "We stopped to smell the flowers and participate in fiestas and siestas."

"So did I," says Sr. Brazil. "I walked twelve hours a day and took more than 6000 pictures."

He tells us he had a child when he was 16 and has worked tirelessly for fifteen years. "My son is now 32. I wanted to walk to clear my life." He, too, is hoping to start anew.

"*Buen Camino* for your new lives," we say to our breakfast companions as we each go our separate ways. We end our Camino with a three-hour bus ride along the coast. It is back to Santiago de Compostela for our flight to Madrid.

At the airport, I pull out my notebook and write:

There is a mysterious energy about walking day after day on a path made sacred by the sweat, blood, tears, and prayers of the millions who have walked before us. The Camino became our home, a place that held us, that provided for us, and a place where, a few times, my heart, mind and soul sang in beautiful harmony. On the Camino, I belonged to a much larger Universe, and there were moments when I felt directly connected to the miracle that is creation.

This walk was not meant to be a search for anything, and yet a whole new world opened up, a magical world, where I could feel the presence of my mum, long dead, walking beside me. The highs of my Camino came from solitude. I fell in love with life. I cannot wait to do another walk and then another one after that. In fact, I want to walk until I die.

My mind is already turning to all the other walking holidays we can do. The Portuguese Camino, the one from Assisi to Rome, the Highland Way in Scotland, and the trek around Mont Blanc immediately come to mind. Maybe we should just move to Europe.

That thought triggers such enthusiasm and excitement, it awakens every voice that lives in my head. *Why not? You've lived in Norway and England and Spain before, so why not again? Besides, what a wonderful escape from American politics. Give Susanna a call, I bet she'd find a place for us to live. This may be the last opportunity in your life to make a major move like this. Who knows what tomorrow holds? Just go for it.* The cacophony of voices is making my head spin. A euphoric spin. I look at David sitting next to me. I let out a groan. *No point even asking him, 'cuz I know what he's going to say.*

One little voice goads, *Go on, ask him.*

"I've been thinking," I say to David. This immediately puts him on high alert. He knows from 43 years of living with me that I'll have some kind of outrageous -- from his perspective -- suggestion that will cause some upheaval of his routine.

"Yeees?" He looks at me.

"What if we move to Europe for a year or eighteen months and just take many walking holidays? Wouldn't that be fun? I mean, who knows how many healthy years we have ahead of us? We have the time and the money." I'm ready to go on and rationalize my suggestion and point out all the advantages and how wonderful it will be, but he cuts me short.

"Why not?" he says.

"Whaaat?" This is not normal. *Don't be so ridiculous!* is what I am expecting to hear. Is this the same David I've known and loved for all these years?

"Why not?" He repeats. "Walking the Camino makes you brave. It's all about putting one foot in front of the other."

For the first time I'm without words or thoughts.

I ponder David's words, and in silence I wonder what this Camino did for me other than getting me addicted to long distance walking. Am I turning into a wise old crone? *Maybe or maybe not,* my brain pipes up. *Don't get delusional and try sipping those dew drops and dancing barefoot in the moonlight. You still have creaky old bones.*

I smile and find myself humming:

'Tis a gift to be simple, 'tis the gift to be free
'Tis a gift to come down where we ought to be.

My princess self did surrender her love for luxury to the utter joy of simplicity and living in the present moment, though I could have done without so many ham and cheese sandwiches. Thank you to the ancient ones who created the myths and legends of Santiago -- wherever he is buried -- and, as a result, created The Way. Thank you to my dear husband for bringing me along.

I tell him that, as I make my head comfortable on his shoulder.

"Did you know that the Monks of Sobrado . . . ."

Like the perfect wife, I listen with only half an ear, so I have no idea what the good monks had to say about the pilgrimage. I drift off into my own world, where my mum is holding me, like she never did in life.

Asifa Kanji

Acknowledgments

My walk on the Camino Del Norte was enriched by all the people whose paths crossed with mine, who shared their stories with me, and hosted David and myself. Thank you, thank you and Buen camino to you all.

I am deeply grateful to my beloved writing group, the Frogs, who encouraged me at every stage of my writing. It is a privilege to be one of you. To the spirit of Sharon - thank you for creating a special place for us to meet every week, and feeding us with your home-made goodies. I miss you so much.

Three people who deserve very special thanks are Andrea Gill, Dennis Read and Ellen Craine. Your feedback on my manuscript was above and beyond the call of friendship. I am incredibly grateful for all your help in shaping this book to what it is.

Lance Bisaccia read the entire manuscript to me. It was a gift I will always treasure. Thank you. Special thanks also to José Javier Pérez López and Ideas Peregrinas, for permission to use your delightful, whimsical maps.

There would have no story to tell if my husband, David, had not enticed me to join him on this walk. There would have been no history included, if it weren't for David's love of learning and sharing, making the journey more meaningful and colorful. To the love of my life, I thank you for all you bring into my life.

Last, but not least, to all my wonderful, faithful readers, thank you for coming on this walk with me.   -Asifa

Also by Asifa Kanji

It's a crazy tale of vampire cats, giant termites and Toyota-flattening freight trains, not to mention playful conjugal text-message sex to pass those weary hours of waiting for the bush taxi. Most of all it is a story of the warm-hearted Malian people, set against a darker background of approaching famine and political unrest, and culminating in the couple's first-hand accounts of the military coup and Peace Corps evacuation from Mali in 2012. Told with humor and compassion, the side-by-side memoirs *300 Cups of Tea* and *The Toughest Job You'll Ever Love* take you on a 14 month journey of life in the Sahel.

Available from Amazon.com

How does a population of 320,000, nearly all of them with common descent from a group of 9th-century Viking settlers, keep their blue-eyed, blonde-haired teenagers from kissing their cousins?

Did you know that beer was banned in Iceland until 1989?

Did you know they have to ask permission from the elves to build roads and tunnels? And if they don't...

These are just some of the warm and funny mysteries you will encounter on that one-of-a-kind island marooned far out on the edge of the Arctic Circle -- Iceland.

Only in Iceland is an irreverent, off-beat, and thoroughly enjoyable collection of her stories. Velkominn!

Available from Amazon.com

Instant Latte

A Tourist in Morocco

Asifa Kanji

Go on a mad whirlwind tour of Morocco with Asifa. Lie naked with her at a Hammam. Get smooched by a camel, bargain for a carpet, dine with her in the homes of local families, and get some insight on this Muslim nation.

What kind of an "authentic experience" does one get in two weeks? "Instant Latte!" she said on Day One. "It's like having your very first café latte made from instant coffee and powdered skimmed milk. It only gives a flash flavor of the real thing."

How wrong she was. Asifa's humorous stories reflect on the effect of tourism on local culture, and the fleeting relationships forged between tourists and their hosts. What a fun, and thoughtful, trip to take with her!

Available from Amazon.com.

About the Author

Asifa Kanji became locally famous by writing long travel letters that people actually like to read. She's traveled in over 50 countries, letting serendipity take her by the hand. She has lived in a mud hut on the edge of the Sahara, in a dilapidated Italian villa in Asmara, in a loft apartment in Oslo. She is a writer, a hiker, a teacher, a henna artist, a Returned Peace Corps Volunteer, and a very good cook. Born in Dar-es-salaam, she grew up in Tanzania and Kenya, was schooled in England, and followed her heart to America in 1975. She lives with her husband and travel companion David, in Ashland, Oregon.

CPSIA information can be obtained
at www.ICGtesting.com
Printed in the USA
LVHW050708090720
660058LV00008B/281